THE
COMPLETE BOOK
OF ASTROLOGY

THE
COMPLETE BOOK
OF ASTROLOGY

Ada Aubin
and June Rifkin

ST. MARTIN'S
ESSENTIALS
NEW YORK

Published in the United States by St. Martin's Essentials,
an imprint of St. Martin's Publishing Group

THE COMPLETE BOOK OF ASTROLOGY. Copyright © 1998, 2022 by The Estate
of Ada Aubin and June Rifkin. All rights reserved. Printed in the United
States of America. For information, address St. Martin's Publishing Group,
120 Broadway, New York, NY 10271.

www.stmartins.com

Designed by Steven Seighman

Library of Congress Cataloging-in-Publication Data

Names: Aubin, Ada, author. | Rifkin, June, author.
Title: The complete book of astrology : an easy-to-use guide to
    astrology that takes you beyond your sun sign and helps you gain
    insight into your personality and potential / Ada Aubin and
    June Rifkin.
Description: First St. Martin's Essentials edition. | New York :
    St. Martin's Essentials, [2022] | Includes index.
Identifiers: LCCN 2021047799 | ISBN 9781250766779
    (trade paperback) | ISBN 9781250766786 (ebook)
Subjects: LCSH: Astrology.
Classification: LCC BF1708.1 .A89 2022 | DDC 133.5—dc23/eng/
    20211029
LC record available at https://lccn.loc.gov/2021047799

Our books may be purchased in bulk for promotional, educational, or
business use. Please contact your local bookseller or the Macmillan
Corporate and Premium Sales Department at 1-800-221-7945, extension
5442, or by email at MacmillanSpecialMarkets@macmillan.com.

First Edition: 2022

10 9 8 7 6 5 4 3 2 1

This book is dedicated to the past masters.
Thank you,
Ada

Contents

Acknowledgments

There are many people to thank for their encouragement, support, and love for Ada throughout her life. Carlos Caro, who spent numerous hours debating the semantics of Ada's choice of words. Truly a brother who could spend hours with his sister over a cup of coffee and a good debate.

Ada was most thankful to her children—Norman, Ada, Rosa, and Michele—who supported her while writing this book, and to her grandchildren, Jason, Christopher, Tony, Nina, Eric, and Ryan.

Never forgotten are the inspiring astrology teachers and mentors, including Lionel Day, Dane Rudhyar, Isabel Hickey, Zipporah Dobyns, and Barbara Watters, as well as all the great and honorable masters who paved the way for modern-day acceptance of astrology and its practitioners.

Lastly, a heartfelt thanks to Ada's dedicated clients, who returned again and again for insight into their lives and possibilities.

—*Michele Aubin (on behalf of Ada Aubin)*

I am pleased to have the opportunity to update this classic book and am excited to see this revised edition emerge to inform and inspire new readers interested in basic astrology. Most of all, I am honored to help maintain Ada Aubin's astrology legacy for decades to come. She was a gifted astrologer whose wisdom and talents are unparalleled. In knowing and working with her, I gained extraordinary insight into my personality, talents, and the unique challenges faced when approaching the crossroads of fate and free will.

I also want to extend my thanks to the following people who were instrumental to this book, past and present: Michele Aubin for her support and assistance; my soul sister Lorraine Bates for introducing me to Ada; my longtime friend and agent, Peter Rubie; my editor, now and then, Keith Kahla, for keeping this literary flame burning; and all the folks at St. Martin's Essentials for making this new edition happen. A shout-out to my three favorite Aries— Stuart, Colin, and Leo—and favorite Sagittarius, Nicholas. And special thoughts to my dear departed friend, teacher, and mentor, Richard Duprey, who helped me hone my craft as a writer. The wisdom he imparted has served me well through the years, and I pay it forward every day.

—*June Rifkin*

An Astrologer's Creed

I sincerely believe . . .

That astrology is a true and divine science and art and, as such, its abuse or misuse would be sacrilegious.

That I must continually strive to be worthy of further enlightenment by the Source of All Knowledge and that I may truly serve Him and my fellow man.

That I will not attempt to guide or advise anyone where my knowledge of astrology shows me it is not for me to do so, as when my own horoscope indicates serious afflictions to another's chart.

That I shall have a sympathetic understanding of the weaknesses of humanity. Never ridiculing, condemning, or becoming accessory before the fact of wrongdoing, I shall endeavor to lift up, encourage, and help as follows:

Where there is ignorance, I will endeavor to enlighten.
Where there is fear, I will encourage confidence and faith.
Where there is hate, I will counsel love.
Where there is error, I will encourage truth.

*Where there are unstable emotions and hysteria, I will
attempt to calm and encourage deliberation.
Where there is sin, I will encourage virtue.
Where there is greed, I will encourage selflessness.*

That if I am not to be a hypocrite, I must live this science to the best of my ability as well as preach it. "For it is
by their works that ye shall know them."

That I shall teach that which I have found to be true, to
all desiring to learn, who are worthy of being taught.

That knowledge in itself is useless unless applied. That
if misapplied, it can be destructive; it must be properly applied.

That properly applied knowledge is wisdom and that
wisdom can free one from so-called "fate."

—*Anonymous*

The Age of Aquarius

In astrological terms, approximately every 2,000- to 2,500-year period represents an "age." Each age is ruled by a sign of the Zodiac and focuses on specific developments in the evolution of mankind. This is demonstrated by archaeological discovery and recorded history. The earliest relevant age would be during the existence of the caveman about ten thousand years ago, during the Age of Leo. The foundations of Egyptian rule, Judaic law, and Oriental philosophy (the Tao) were set during the Age of Taurus (4000–2000 BC, approximately). The Age of Aries (2000 BC to AD 1) brought both conflict and intellectual advancement. Aries, a fire sign, ruled the age when ancient Greece was in its glory, Moses led the Jews out of Egypt, and Rome was building its vast empire. It was also an age of artistic and philosophical expression and discovery. The birth of Christ signified the beginning of the Age of Pisces (AD 1–2000), and appropriately, Pisces is the sign of fishes, a symbol equated with Christianity. This age gave rise to religion, vision, and spirituality. As Pisces is the twelfth (and last) sign of the Zodiac, it brings a fusion and culmination of all that has come before it.

Although the pop group The 5th Dimension sang about it in the 1960s, only now are we experiencing the "dawning of the Age of Aquarius." Technically, the Aquarian Age begins sometime between the years 2000–2500, depending on the source, but its anticipation decades ago inspired a hit song written for the smash Broadway musical *Hair*, which reflected the emerging and idealistic hippie culture of peace and love. It was also the time when astrology became accessible and popular with the masses.

Baby boomers may recall, with either nostalgia or embarrassment, parading around in bell-bottoms and Nehru jackets asking, "What's your sign?" of everyone they met. Most were probably unaware of what it meant to be a Taurus or Sagittarius—touting your sign was simply a conversation starter, especially when socializing and dating. Knowledge of astrology was generally limited to personality traits of the Sun Signs and those with whom you were compatible. Daily and monthly horoscopes were popularized in newspapers and magazines, with readers trying to make the brief and general predictions fit their lives.

Sometime in the 1980s, the astrology craze waned, and its practitioners and enthusiasts quietly retreated from the public eye. They remained engaged and committed, however, and as computers began to facilitate the once time-consuming drawing of birth charts and calculation of transits, slowly yet steadily, astrology emerged again.

As the Aquarian Age dawns, the world is undergoing great and rapid advancement in communication, information, and technology—all Aquarian in nature. These changes are both exciting—due to how our smartphones connect us to everything and everyone globally—but also frightening due to issues of privacy, security, and a bombardment of content that can be stressful. Aquarius is a mental sign seeking balance. Without balance, there can be no growth—body, mind, and soul must function in unison. Since entering the twenty-first century, many people have turned to yoga, meditation, and similar practices to cope with stress and create personal balance. There has also been a rising interest in personal growth and tools that can support self-awareness.

Astrology can offer knowledge to promote self-awareness. It can map for us those ways or roads that are most relevant and productive. The birth chart reveals the many facets of an individual's personality, character, and potential, along with insight and opportunity for self-discovery, career, relationships, and other personal goals. It can make sense of the senseless or chaotic and provide structure, purpose, and, most valuably, promise.

It has been said that when the student is ready, the teacher appears. For anyone with a genuine interest or curiosity who wishes to explore and study the wondrous complexities of this ancient craft, this book exists to feed the mind, explore the past, present, and future of astrology, and offer insight and information on this complex and fascinating subject. It's time to shed old and distorted impressions—astrologers do *not* parade around in beads and caftans and have crystal balls—and to take a renewed look at this complex body of knowledge that has existed and been used since early man beheld the sky and stars above him.

Through the study of astrology, the Age of Aquarius can prove to be a hopeful, humane, and transformational time. It begins simply, with an open and curious mind.

1

What Is Astrology?

Astrology is both an art form and a science—the "science of possibilities." It deals with the effects that the planets (including the Sun and the Moon) have on humans. The interaction between planets and a person born at a given time has been set into a system that explains, with accuracy, their potential. A birth chart, or horoscope, is a personal road map that provides clear-cut and compelling explanations for the challenges a person can face.

Astrology has withstood the test of time and, as a result, has embodied and undertaken the delineation of human nature. The configuration of symbols and signs in a birth chart can help to time and understand events in your life. It provides insight into relationships, family, career, and, most importantly, the potentials and limitations of an individual.

Astrology deals with both mental and physical maturation. It holds the key to correcting attitudes that affect your life. The objective of studying and understanding astrology is to provide and produce self-awareness. It is challenging to attain complete self-awareness, but the rewards bring harmony and balance into our lives. Awareness of ourselves ultimately enhances our objectivity about life and how we relate to and interact with others. Astrology is an excellent diagnostic tool that can assist us in achieving the desired objectivity.

THE HISTORY OF ASTROLOGY

The history of astrology is as old as the history of man. The need to relate to the cosmos was common to all ancient civilizations. Some bits and pieces of artifacts that predate recorded history were used in rituals to worship the heavenly bodies. Early man needed to place himself within the context of the vast universe. He was a tireless observer who was aware of his vulnerability.

The high priest or priestess was the selected person who would devote his or her life to the study and practice of this knowledge. It was serious business, as the entire culture depended on such a person, such as the Native American medicine man.

The genesis of astrology is unknown, but all cultures claim it. The I Ching of the Chinese has astrology based on Moon cycles. The Kabbalah represents the work of the Jewish mystics. Egypt left monuments to its astrological practices, as have the Islamic world and the cultures of ancient Greece and Rome. Even Europe collected and held astrological knowledge in high position, clear to the Middle Ages.

Astrology, as a mystical science, represents the development of the human psyche. This body of knowledge grows and changes as the human being undergoes his evolution. The notion that astrology is a religion has led many to fear and misunderstand this excellent diagnostic tool. Astrology has coexisted with the dogmatic faiths for centuries without difficulty. The Torah does not deny the Kabbalah but confirms it. The I Ching doesn't contradict the Tao but enhances it.

The political/religious developments throughout Europe during and after the Middle Ages sent astrology underground. The great astrologer and clairvoyant Michel de Nostradamus wrote his prophecies in metaphoric quatrains, using a language that combined Latin and old French, as a subterfuge to avoid being accused of heresy by the church. This was when the infamous side of astrology was born. This powerful tool became used as a weapon. This knowledge gave an advantage to those who used it for personal gain. During World War II, Adolf Hitler employed astrologers in hopes of outsmarting the Allies; little did he know the Allies were using astrologers to outflank him. This selfish motive backfired, since "service to others" is a prepossession that an astrologer does not violate.

The introduction of psychiatry into modern culture relegated astrology to being a "poor relation." Psychiatrists have studied human nature and, in so doing, have coined a language that has expanded the definitions of planets and circumstances found in a chart. One cannot help but see the approaching union between these two sciences.

Carl Jung, the renowned Swiss psychologist and student of Sigmund Freud, took astrology seriously. He philosophically separated from Freud as he studied the subject and pursued psychology on a separate and independent level. He believed in *synchronicity*, which is the concept that certain events on Earth, both global and personal, coincide in time with similar planetary relations in astronomy. Jung coined the terms *collective unconscious* and *archetypes*, which also describe the purpose and significance of astrology. Michel Gauquelin, a French psychologist and statistician, studied and wrote of how the positions of the planets in a birth chart reflected the personality and profession of an individual.

The contributions to astrology are endless. This ancient body of knowledge is vast and, when properly used, can provide an insight into the personality like no other tool. In the Aquarian Age, the quest is to discover our authentic personalities, not just live with the ones constructed for us. It is a time for enlightenment so that we may avoid the mistakes of the past.

PREDESTINATION VERSUS FREE WILL

The discussion of predestination versus free will has a long history. The school of thought that states that we are wholly responsible for our actions cannot explain the many occurrences that are out of context in our lives. The study of an astrological chart directs and points out the objectives and goals of our lives. It is quite easy to foresee or experience a transit—a planet that triggers another planet restricts us to that phase or lesson. The response can occur at three levels, depending on one's spiritual development: at the physical level, with all its apparent manifestations; at the emotional level, subjecting oneself to psychic traumas; or at the theoretical level, where one can, through love and patience, transcend the growing pains experienced.

When this knowledge is placed within the framework of a natal chart, the planets and the signs in their given houses deliver an inevitable lesson. The empty houses represent free will. How free? The opportunity to use empty houses is important, particularly when part of a T-square. In that configuration, there will be leakage, wasted energy, or perhaps an opportunity to untangle the difficulties of such a hard aspect.

Astrology accepts the concept that we choose our parents, our economic level, our race, and in our collective unconscious, the knowledge of past lives. This "package" of choices helps to advance our souls. Sometimes we must also go back in order to undo past mistakes. By doing so, we progress to the next level of development.

This opportunity for advancement can be disrupted by a personality that changes in midstream. For example, the alcoholic or drug addict may drop out of society and stop his chart, but this only acts as a delay. The individual will come back and repeat that life until he has overcome the action, each time having to face the value of life and living in various modes.

Although a case can be made for predestination, the recognition of free will figures strongly into the equation. Great sadness is suffered when the will is broken. The difficulty that such a person experiences sometimes leads to heights of accomplishment. Yet for another person, it becomes his undoing. In the end, each person must balance his life. He must strike when it is in his power to do so and allow the universe to take over when it is out of his hands.

As noted time and time again within astrological circles, "The stars impel, they do not compel."

2

Elements of Astrology

THE ZODIAC

The Zodiac is a belt of fixed stars that circle Earth. The correlation between these stars, the seasons, and human behavior evolved into the study of astrology.

The Zodiac is comprised of twelve constellations, or signs, each spanning thirty degrees. Each of these signs spans about four weeks per calendar year. The latitude and longitude of the birth chart will determine the number of degrees in a house or the sign that appears in a given house. This backdrop of stars for the travel of the Sun Sign describes its archetype. As in astronomy, the positions of clustered stars define the various constellations seen in the sky and are named for the patterns they make. Each of the twelve signs of the Zodiac reflects its corresponding ancient constellation.

The symbols or *glyphs* assigned to the constellations have varied points of origin. Egypt, ancient Greece, China, and India have influenced the system that is now used as a shorthand. The study of ancient cultures will enrich the knowledge of the Zodiac, as these constellations and symbols were not born out of a simplistic look at the sky but out of a need in each culture for humans to understand their place in the scheme of creation. As each planet moves through the Zodiac, it travels from sign to sign, taking on a different trait in each placement.

SIGNS OF THE ZODIAC

The twelve signs of the Zodiac are:

Aries	Ram	♈	Rules First House
Taurus	Bull	♉	Rules Second House
Gemini	Twins	♊	Rules Third House
Cancer	Crab	♋	Rules Fourth House
Leo	Lion	♌	Rules Fifth House
Virgo	Virgin	♍	Rules Sixth House
Libra	Scales	♎	Rules Seventh House
Scorpio	Scorpion	♏	Rules Eighth House
Sagittarius	Centaur/Archer	♐	Rules Ninth House
Capricorn	Goat	♑	Rules Tenth House
Aquarius	Water Bearer	♒	Rules Eleventh House
Pisces	Fish	♓	Rules Twelfth House

The signs and their unique characteristics will be covered in detail when we explore the Sun Signs in chapter 4.

THE PLANETS

The field of astrology is influenced by ten planets, including the Sun and the Moon (which are not really planets but, respectively, a star and a satellite of Earth). These planets, their transits, and their relationships to Earth are studied to determine the personalities and potentials of every individual. The planets are basically raw energy. We are affected by such energy in the way we choose to respond to or ignore it.

Sun	☉	Jupiter	♃
Moon	☽	Saturn	♄
Mercury	☿	Uranus	♅
Venus	♀	Neptune	♆
Mars	♂	Pluto	♇

Since the Sun, Moon, Mercury, Venus, and Mars move quickly and are close to each other, they are considered *personal planets*. These planets take about two years to complete their orbits and have a more personal and noticeable impact on our lives.

Jupiter and Saturn are *viewpoint planets*. Their orbits span a greater length of time and impact the transition of decades upon our lives.

Uranus, Neptune, and Pluto are *outer*, or *transpersonal*, *planets*. This group of planets has a more generational rather than personal influence.

The placement of planets in a birth chart and their movement give depth to a horoscope, taking it beyond the analysis of the Sun Sign.

RETROGRADE PLANETS

A retrograde action is a planet slowing down. In contrast to the velocity of Earth, it appears to be going backward. No planet ever goes backward or leaves its orbit. It is always moving forward. The apparent backward motion of a retrograde is simply the loss of velocity. The Sun and Moon never go into retrograde motion.

Retrograde planets represent work that must be achieved in this lifetime because it was not accomplished or reconciled in a past life.

THE HOUSES

As Earth completes one full rotation in a twenty-four-hour day, the whole Zodiac passes over it. As the signs divide the Zodiac into twelve four-week segments of the year, the houses divide it into twelve two-hour periods of the day. The first house, which begins approximately at dawn, rests on the ascendant or eastern horizon. Each house represents a different facet of life as well as personal and public conditions.

First House

The first house cusp represents the first cardinal point. It is the entrance of the ego and deals with the self. When there are planets in this house, it indicates that you must reconcile your ego. If there are no planets there, it indicates that there is no ego problem.

The first house is also the house of your ascendant or rising sign, as well as your ego. It represents your appearance, your best foot forward, and what you project to others. It represents your personality and your outlook. Personal actions, personal instincts—those things that belong to the self are in this first house.

Second House

The second house is personal concepts and ideas. It is also the house of resources. It is the fashion in which you display values and personal obligations, such as earning, spending, and establishing your financial standing.

Third House

The third house is communications. It is also the house of memories. It is also the house associated with learning—either the ability to learn or the misfortune of learning (or mental) difficulties.

This is the house of siblings. It is also the house associated with short-term transportation and local travel.

Fourth House

The fourth house is associated with the soul's inheritance, family, and the home. It represents nurturing, roots, and, most importantly, our mothers. Your inheritance from your mother enters in the fourth house.

This is also the house of beginning and ending and the entrance of the soul. People with prominent planets in the fourth house deal with real estate and property.

Fifth House

The fifth house is the house of talent and procreation, whether it be children, self-esteem, or creative forces and endeavors. The fifth house is also the house of romance, fun, drama, physical outlets, and self-expression.

Sixth House

The sixth house is the environment. It is also the house of health. Your internal and external environment work together or against each other to impact your health.

This house represents not only the environment of the home but also your work environment and employment.

The sixth house represents your ambitions as well as service to others.

Seventh House

The seventh house is the descendant point, the opposite point of the rising or ascendant point. The seventh house is where sociability is displayed, including your partners, and where you balance your ego with the egos of others.

This is the house where open enemies and competitors will arise. It is also the house of partnerships, relationships, marriages, legal partnerships, and cooperation.

Eighth House

The eighth house is the other house of partnerships because it opposes the second house: my ideas versus your ideas. You bring to any relationship not just your ego but also concepts and ideas. You have a background, a history, a standard. You have a whole procedure that has been part of your life, and when you take on a partner, you must reconcile your standards with your partner's standards.

This house has always been associated with sexuality and psychic sexual energy.

It is also both the house of inheritances and the house of great losses. Many people with planets in the eighth house tend to lose their inheritances.

Ninth House

The ninth house is the elevation of the mind. It is considered the house of higher education—not only formal education, religion, or philosophy but also abstract knowledge. Through the ninth house, you acquire an understanding that forms your attitude.

The ninth house is the house of teaching, education, and publishing. It is also the house of in-laws and long journeys.

Tenth House

The tenth house is the house of duties, responsibilities, personal status—it represents what has been done with what you acquired in the fourth house. In the tenth house, you will be judged. You will have a whole lifetime to take your inheritance and translate it into what the world will judge as success or failure.

The tenth house is the house of the father. It is the house of prestige and career, reputation, and law.

Eleventh House

The eleventh house is sorting. It sorts out who your friends and associates are, what you have done with your creativity—in essence, what you have accomplished. It is the house of goals and objectives.

The eleventh house represents the groups, associations, and people you deal with and the responsibility to or association with the children of others, whether it be as a teacher or stepparent. The eleventh house also relates to your social responsibility.

Twelfth House

The twelfth house is the last and ultimate house and has always been feared because it is both the house of confinement and the house of the greatest depth of creativity, knowledge, and resources. It is the house of the soul's transformation. If you flow with the twelfth house, it can be an excellent source for tapping a reservoir of information, knowledge, and past-life contact.

The objective of the twelfth house is to confine your ego because your ego must transmute. It must mature, develop, and rise beyond narcissistic pleasures and desires to acquire what it wants. The conflict between what you need and what you want can be destructive to the soul. This is the house of karma or the end of it.

The twelfth house also rules hospitals and institutions.

HOUSE POSITIONS

Angular Houses

If planets in a chart come off an angle—that means in the first, fourth, seventh, or tenth house position—those planets are powerful and active, and will work overtly.

If you have many angular planets in your chart, it means that you have been assigned a task that distinguishes you from your generation. You are going to either be far more advanced or in charge of current or subsequent generations.

Succedent Houses

If many planets in your chart are placed in the second, fifth, eighth, and eleventh house positions, they will impact your emotions and desires.

Cadent Houses

If many planets in your chart are placed in the third, sixth, ninth, and twelfth house positions, they will have a more subliminal influence, most noticeably in mental energy.

THE NATURAL ZODIAC

The "natural" Zodiac begins with Aries, which coincides with the vernal equinox or first day of spring. Aries appears on and rules the first cusp (ascendant) and the first house of the natural Zodiac, which, when placed on a "wheel," appears on the eastern horizon.

HEMISPHERES

The lower or southern hemisphere, which goes from Aries to Cancer to Libra, has significance in a chart. The signs of this hemisphere tend to be primitive. When planets are placed in this hemisphere, it means that, sooner or later, you will go through a period of introspection.

From Aries to the north position of Capricorn to Libra is the upper or northern hemisphere. The signs of this hemisphere tend to be complex. The houses here are more outward and extroverted. When planets are placed in this hemisphere, you will interact with others.

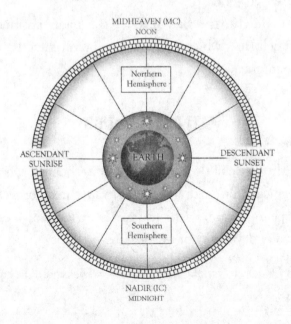

ASCENDANT, MIDHEAVEN, DESCENDANT, AND NADIR

The significant points in the daily cycle are when the Sun rises, culminates, sets, and anti-culminates.

The ascendant appears on the cusp of the first house, occurring at sunrise. This position reflects your personality and who you are to the outside world.

The midheaven, or medium coeli (MC), is reached at around noon and occupies the highest point of a chart. Embodied in that position reflects what you have become and how you are perceived and judged by the world.

The descendant point occurs when the Sun has reached the sunset position.

At midnight, the Sun reaches the nadir position, or imum coeli (IC), which is the lowest point, directly opposite the midheaven.

QUADRANTS

When the circle of the natural Zodiac is squared, it creates four segments, or quadrants, containing three consecutive houses per quadrant. Each quadrant has a focus on a particular area of development in your life:

First Quadrant (1st, 2nd, 3rd Houses) = Focuses on the ego and the self

Second Quadrant (4th, 5th, 6th Houses) = Focuses on awareness outside the self and toward family and friends
Third Quadrant (7th, 8th, 9th Houses) = Focuses on relationships and partnerships
Fourth Quadrant (10th, 11th, 12th Houses) = Focuses on humanity and society at large

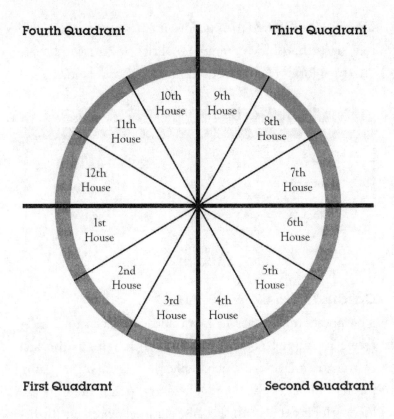

Fourth Quadrant

Third Quadrant

10th House
9th House
11th House
8th House
12th House
7th House
1st House
6th House
2nd House
5th House
3rd House
4th House

First Quadrant

Second Quadrant

When viewing a birth chart, look at how many planets are placed in each quadrant. Some charts are balanced; others have an abundance of planets in one or two quadrants.

The quadrants that contain the most planets indicate the areas of focus that are significant to your emotional and spiritual development.

CROSSES (QUADRUPLICITIES)

Crosses, also referred to as quadruplicities or modalities, are four signs that share common qualities. In astrology, there are three kinds of crosses: cardinal, fixed, and mutable.

CARDINAL	FIXED	MUTABLE
Aries	Taurus	Gemini
Cancer	Leo	Virgo
Libra	Scorpio	Sagittarius
Capricorn	Aquarius	Pisces

Cardinal Cross

The points from Aries to Libra and Capricorn to Cancer create a cardinal point or cardinal cross. This is the first of the three crosses or quadruplicities. *Cardinal*, in Latin, means "hinges of the door." These four points are essential for developing the psyche because cardinal represents the beginning, the opening of the door to a new path. These four points work toward initiating something, whether it be the evolution of a personality or a soul.

Cardinal signs tend to be initiators by nature. They are champions of causes that can benefit their fellow man.

Fixed Cross

The fixed cross is commonly called the *cross of the soul*. The four signs of the fixed cross are Taurus, Leo, Scorpio, and Aquarius. These signs tend to be inflexible, particularly in their opinions.

The fixed signs carry an innate fear of rejection and a morbid dread of change. They find it difficult to alter emotions, and they also hold grudges. To evolve spiritually and maintain physical well-being, they must find methods of release and heal old wounds.

Mutable Cross

The third cross is the mutable cross or the *common cross*. It represents whether your paths—your chosen paths—have any value or if you have outgrown them.

The four signs of the mutable cross are Gemini, Virgo, Sagittarius, and Pisces. The mutable signs are usually flexible and adaptable by nature. But they can also be volatile, changeable, and inconsistent and should be handled in a healthy way to avoid detrimental effects on the central nervous system.

In esoteric astrology, where the concept of past lives is addressed, the mutable cross is usually indicative of lifetimes spent in churches or as men (or women) of the cloth. As a result, mutable signs often carry a sense of inhibition and introspection.

THE ELEMENTS (TRIPLICITIES)

The elements, also referred to as *triplicities*, represent a method of operation for the Sun Sign. There are four elements—fire, earth, air, and water—with three Sun Signs in each element.

FIRE	EARTH	AIR	WATER
Aries	Taurus	Gemini	Cancer
Leo	Virgo	Libra	Scorpio
Sagittarius	Capricorn	Aquarius	Pisces

Fire

The three fire signs are Aries, Leo, and Sagittarius. Fire represents the will. The will is the spirit within an individual. It is enthusiastic, directed energy. Fire is always looking for a challenge and taking spirited action for the benefit of the self.

Earth

The three earth signs are Taurus, Virgo, and Capricorn. Earth represents structure and that which is solid and tangible. It represents the senses. Earth signs deal with the material world comfortably. They have an innately suspicious attitude toward the unseen, so they rely on their senses—touch, taste, smell, sight, and hearing—for confirmation.

Air

The three air signs are Gemini, Libra, and Aquarius. Air represents concepts, ideas, and abstract expression. These concepts are expressed through many forms—painting, sculpture, writing, and the like. Air signs are idea people. They are involved with their ideas but not with their emotions.

Water

The three water signs are Cancer, Scorpio, and Pisces. Water can be a difficult but potentially wonderful element. Water, unlike any of the other elements, lacks consistency. It will take the form and shape of the vessel that holds it. Water represents intuition and the ability to feel. The water signs tend to understand and deal with other people's feelings.

BALANCE OF ELEMENTS

If you take the ten planets in your chart and note the signs in which they are placed, you can then determine the balance of the four elements. Having one or no planets in any element indicates a lack; having four or more planets in any element indicates an abundance.

It is interesting to note that when a person lacks an element in his chart, he will invariably be attracted to someone who possesses that which he lacks.

Lack of Fire / Too Much Fire

The lack of fire indicates a broken will. This person is vulnerable because lacking fire indicates that he doesn't have joie de vivre, the enthusiasm that makes life wonderful. His quest in life is to devise a method by which he can display his will.

Having too much fire creates a tenacious individual. His willfulness and inflexibility cast an overbearing attitude over every challenge he encounters. This quality is challenging for relationships because this individual's need to do as he sees fit can stampede over somebody else's life.

Lack of Earth / Too Much Earth

A lack of earth signs creates insecurity. This person does not feel grounded and lacks the consistency needed to produce mastery. He usually loses faith in what he is doing and doesn't turn the corner to see success on the other side. This is the individual who can quit just before he wins.

Too much earth produces self-reliance and security that borders on laziness. This individual is constructive and confident in his work and other practical activities to provide himself with the security he needs. However, this can be an unimaginative individual who, although consistent, successful, and a potentially good earner, will not be the type who will venture into any kind of speculation or risk.

Lack of Air / Too Much Air

If air is lacking in a chart, it produces a need for learning and a search for concepts. This individual is considered a borderline genius—his quest for knowledge ultimately produces a bright, intelligent person.

Too much air in a chart creates a woolly headed individual who spins ideas and concepts but doesn't get anything up off the drawing board. There is too much thought and not enough action to complete or conquer anything.

Lack of Water / Too Much Water

An individual who lacks water in his chart cannot empathize or understand the feelings of others. He creates emotional scenes to produce sensations, making him callous and unapproachable.

On the other hand, having too much water cripples a person because he becomes soaked—literally inundated by his emotions. This individual is not just overwhelmed by his feelings but is also stimulated by the feelings of others, leaving himself vulnerable, and his emotional energy and resources sapped.

Balanced Elements

The individual with a relatively balanced chart (any combination of 3/2/3/2) will revert to his own needs in a crisis. He will find his equilibrium and then act.

COMBINATIONS OF ELEMENTS

Many charts display a predominance of two elements. The combination of these elements will impact the motivations and actions of an individual.

Fire/Air

All fire and air signs are masculine/extroverts, so the high concepts of air and the will of fire make for a forward-moving person who can promote his thoughts and ideas. This individual might have strong verbal ability, like a lawyer, or might have an optimistic, almost humorous attitude about life.

Water/Earth

This is an easy combination. When water and earth are emphasized, there is an ability to harness the power of emotions. Earth confines, giving structure and form to water and hence, emotions. The result is a creativity that allows water/earth to be expressive and artistic.

Air/Water

The air/water combination is challenging because these two elements are in direct opposition to each other. Earth is passive and feminine; air is masculine and intellectually aggressive. The energies of each element are so distinctly different that when these elements combine, they begin to create odd combinations. At the most positive level, an air/

water combination can develop a type of feeling/intuition that can lead to some degree of comfort.

When the intuition of water combines with the concepts of air, it begins to create ideas that are worthwhile and satisfying to both those elements. If the physical and psychological difficulties created by these incongruous elements are overcome, this combination can produce an imaginative and skilled individual who can deal with people effectively and thrive in the healing arts.

Earth/Air

The combination of earth and air creates a contradictory push/pull. Earth is grounded and tangible, while air is lofty, rising above everyday circumstances. When these elements combine, they create an individual who has one foot in each camp and is not quite sure who and what he is and how he is supposed to operate. When harmony is achieved between earth and air, it develops the ability to sort out those concepts and notions of value. Since air produces many ideas, earth will take these ideas and give them structure and balance.

An earth/air person tends to distrust impulses and emotionalism—he thinks in a broad but concise way. This is an individual who can distribute wealth, commodities, and materials, and work hard to take care of loved ones.

Fire/Water

The combination of fire/water is highly combustible. When water is heated by fire, it bubbles and boils. This is a person who becomes impulsive, who acts on his feelings, whether right or wrong. Emotions overshadow logic.

The individual with this combination is extremely sensitive and worried about what others think. He needs to sell himself and explain to the world who he is and what he is about. He suffers emotional swings because there is a conflict between water's need for security—needing to hang on and bond—and fire's ego, which simply wants to go forth.

With discipline, this individual can accomplish a great deal if he expresses his emotions without losing perimeters. At his worst, however, this person is a little firecracker, exploding all over the place because of deep, internal frustration. It is difficult to control these mood swings, and they can lead to troubled relationships.

Earth/Fire

The combination of earth and fire results in what noted astrologer Zipporah Dobyns referred to as "the steamroller." This individual has enormous drive and a need to act. He will either spring into action over an idea or, if he discovers that it has no practical value, eliminate it. The creative energy of fire mixed with the plotting and planning of earth is a successful combination. This person can take a small business and turn it into a large, successful business. He possesses enormous faith and patience in all undertakings, believing that everything planned and acted upon will eventually be realized.

On the other hand, if the energy created by the earth/fire combination is not disciplined, the negative side of this steamroller will emerge to challenge and trample on the ideas of others. He must learn to accept that there are different ways of doing things and that "different" doesn't necessarily mean better or worse, right or wrong. His productivity is admirable, but his sensitivity needs to be improved.

GROUPS

The signs of the Zodiac can also be classified into groups— emotional, intellectual, and theoretical. Each group consists of four signs, one of each element—fire, earth, air, and water.

EMOTIONAL	INTELLECTUAL	THEORETICAL
Aries	Leo	Sagittarius
Taurus	Virgo	Capricorn
Gemini	Libra	Aquarius
Cancer	Scorpio	Pisces

The Emotional Group
There are four signs in the emotional group—Aries, Taurus, Gemini, and Cancer—which are also the first four signs of the Zodiac. Signs of the emotional group are unable to control their emotions before speaking or acting. Even when they strive to handle things at an intellectual level, their

emotions come through. If the signs of this group begin suppressing their emotions, psychosomatic illnesses will develop.

The emotional group must learn to displace emotions, to think, and then react. This is the *I* group. Its objective is to learn to identify the self.

The Intellectual Group

The intellectual group consists of Leo, Virgo, Libra, and Scorpio, the four middle signs of the Zodiac. This group takes its thinking, responses, and emotions and filters everything through its intellect. The signs in this group tell you how they think, not how they feel, because they don't have contact with their feelings. They disassociate themselves from their emotions in order to intellectualize.

Members of this group need to stop thinking and to act. Otherwise, they'll sit and pontificate on the ramifications of everything without ever responding or moving.

The intellectual group is the *we* group. They are concerned with others, and they have partnerships—somebody else's ego is involved in this intellectualizing. They can take things from their head, filter them through the gut, and succeed for themselves and others.

The Theoretical Group

The theoretical group includes the signs of Sagittarius, Capricorn, Aquarius, and Pisces, the last four signs of the Zodiac. This is the most complicated group of the three—their illnesses are worse, and their actions can be extreme. When they are positive, they can be superb and reach enormous heights; when they are negative, they can go completely down the tubes.

Theoretical signs take their emotions, and instead of intellectualizing, they transcend them. They live in the world of ought to be, could be, and should be—these signs can "should" you to death. The inherent difficulty for the theoretical group is dealing with "what is." When you talk to theoretical signs about an issue, just when you thought you had explained how things are, they'll go off on a tangent of what could, should, ought to be, and may be, and forget about what is. They need to learn the law of cause and effect. They must learn to practice what they preach to others.

This group is considered the *universal* group. Their egos are satisfied and developed by the responses of large groups—institutions, corporations, and so on.

GENDER

The signs of the Zodiac are classified by gender, alternating between masculine and feminine, every other sign. In some texts, the signs can be classified as positive or negative, active or passive, extroverted or introverted, and yin versus yang. The various terminologies associated with gender quality can be confusing. Positive/negative does not mean good/bad. Furthermore, a woman in a masculine sign does not lack femininity any more than a man in a feminine sign lacks masculinity.

For example, Libra, a masculine sign, is ruled by Venus, a planet of refinement, beauty, and femininity; Scorpio, a feminine sign, is aggressive and powerful, traits often considered masculine. *Please note: These so-called gender or masculine/feminine qualities are how signs have been defined traditionally. As such, these definitions will be maintained throughout the book.*

There is always a striving for balance between opposing traits. However, men and women in opposite gender signs often face certain challenges that are determined and influenced by the rest of the natal chart. These influences will be addressed and illustrated in greater detail in the Sun Signs chapter.

The qualities of masculine and feminine also apply to the influence of one's parents. The six masculine signs of Aries, Gemini, Leo, Libra, Sagittarius, and Aquarius are considered "father dominated." If you were born under one of these Sun Signs, you came into this life to deal with and work out issues with your father. Those issues are not necessarily good or bad. It only means that through maturation, you must come to terms with Dad.

The same is true of the six feminine signs—Taurus, Cancer, Virgo, Scorpio, Capricorn, and Pisces. If you are born under one of these Sun Signs, you will deal with and work out issues relating to your mother.

The Sun, which represents the father, is the chosen destiny you are here to work out and fulfill. The Moon, which represents the mother, personifies your physical and emotional inheritance that leads to your medical history or karma. This is of particular influence if your Moon is placed in the fourth house.

MOON NODES AND POLARITIES

Within a natal chart, besides planets and signs, are nodes. These are imaginary lines that represent the path of the Moon when it is circling Earth. The Moon crosses at two points in its course—the first is called the North Node (☊), or Dragon's Head, and the second is called the South Node (☋), or Dragon's Tail. These points, which oppose each other, are karmic and important. The North Node represents movement and fulfillment, while the South Node represents complacency and old habits. Both the North and the South Nodes are always in retrograde action and must be reconciled or else they will create frustration. Since human beings cannot always reach a middle ground, they tend to go toward either one node or the other. A balance must be struck between the pull of the North and South Nodes to establish well-centeredness.

Aries/Libra Polarity

Aries/Libra is self-will versus personal freedom. It is also the reconciliation between your ego and the ego of others. The fiery Mars quality of Aries versus the passive Venus quality of Libra pulls back and forth. When you have a South Node in Aries/North Node in Libra, you already know the consequences of aggression. The reconciliation is not being passive but knowing when to use aggression and when to exhibit passivity. If you have a South Node in Libra/North Node in Aries, you will understand the consequences of indifference. Many times, passivity is interpreted as indifference.

When this polarity is in balance, and aggression and passivity are successfully integrated, Aries/Libra can become an excellent therapist or counselor because he innately understands the conflict of one's internal forces.

Taurus/Scorpio Polarity

The Taurus/Scorpio polarity represents self-indulgence and material possessions versus the value and respect of others. In Taurus, there is a tendency to give it all away versus Scorpio, which is always holding back. Scorpio is secretive and doesn't feel that he should inform you—if you don't know something, educate yourself.

If this polarity is integrated, it can help others to recognize their self-worth. People with this polarity can be at the top of their abilities, particularly in careers related to finance or research.

Gemini/Sagittarius Polarity

The polarity of Gemini/Sagittarius is the self versus others. Gemini gathers information while Sagittarius processes information. When balanced, it integrates words with concepts, creating knowledge. These are referred to as *the teaching nodes*. When integrated, this makes for a great communicator.

Cancer/Capricorn Polarity

The polarity of Cancer/Capricorn is home versus economic life. It can be quite a pull, but an important one because it creates a tension between security and responsibility. The Cancer/Capricorn polarity usually represents past-life starvation. That starvation through Capricorn can be a business failure or inability to succeed; through Cancer, it can be actual deprivation and starvation. Anxiety is inherent in this polarity, as well as a need to integrate. A home business is a good option when this polarity is prominent.

Leo/Aquarius Polarity

The polarity of Leo/Aquarius is self-awareness versus the humanistic concern for others. This polarity is pushing and pulling between getting out of the self and unto others or retreating entirely within the self. When integrated, this polarity allows an individual to mingle, exchange ideas, and not lose the self, which can result in personal growth and achievement.

Virgo/Pisces Polarity

In the polarity of Virgo/Pisces, Virgo analyzes the parts while Pisces sees the whole picture. One must know what the components are to master the inner peace that can come from knowing. There is a patient-versus-doctor quality to this polarity—both signs are healers, both are communicators, both have sensitivity and knowledge. When integrated, this is an excellent polarity for doctors or any profession that involves the care or healing of others.

ZODIACAL SIGN ATTRIBUTES

SIGN	RULER	ELEMENT	CROSS	GROUP	GENDER	POLARITY
Aries	Mars	Fire	Cardinal	Emotional	Masculine	Libra
Taurus	Venus	Earth	Fixed	Emotional	Feminine	Scorpio
Gemini	Mercury	Air	Mutable	Emotional	Masculine	Sagittarius
Cancer	Moon	Water	Cardinal	Emotional	Feminine	Capricorn
Leo	Sun	Fire	Fixed	Intellectual	Masculine	Aquarius
Virgo	Mercury	Earth	Mutable	Intellectual	Feminine	Pisces
Libra	Venus	Air	Cardinal	Intellectual	Masculine	Aries
Scorpio	Pluto/Mars	Water	Fixed	Intellectual	Feminine	Taurus
Sagittarius	Jupiter	Fire	Mutable	Theoretical	Masculine	Gemini
Capricorn	Saturn	Earth	Cardinal	Theoretical	Feminine	Cancer
Aquarius	Uranus/Saturn	Air	Fixed	Theoretical	Masculine	Leo
Pisces	Neptune/Jupiter	Water	Mutable	Theoretical	Feminine	Virgo

3

The Astrological Chart

WHAT IS A HOROSCOPE?

The natal horoscope, or birth chart, is a diagram in the form of a "wheel" that depicts the placement in the sky of signs, planets, and houses at the time of your birth. All these factors, taken together, reflect your unique personality, potential, and possible path of endeavor. A horoscope can be determined for any occurrence—a marriage, a business, even the birth of a nation.

Horoscopes that appear in newspapers and magazines consider factors influencing the Sun Signs. It is a broad perspective that assumes that everyone born under the same sign will act, respond, and experience events in a similar way. This is not the case. Though you can determine much by a thorough examination of your Sun Sign, how many times have you met someone who shared your sign but with whom you had little in common? Although you have the same Sun Sign, you will most likely have different rising signs and Moon, Mercury, or Venus placements. People born under the same Sun Sign do share some basic characteristics, but *all* the planets in context make each and every one of us a pure individual in our own right.

CREATING A BIRTH CHART

In today's high-tech world, the simplest and most accurate way to construct a birth chart is by computer. What took hours for the novice to calculate by hand is now available within minutes. In fact, even the most accomplished astrologers use them so that they can focus on interpreting the chart rather than drawing it.

Constructing a chart by hand is not only time-consuming, but the task cannot be undertaken without the availability or purchase of several other books and resources that provide the information necessary for accurate chart construction. These resources include an ephemeris, a book that lists the positions of all the planets, from either a noon or midnight perspective, for any given month, day, and year; a book or website that provides the longitude and latitude of any city/state/country of birth; and a "table of houses," which gives the cusps of the houses for the degrees of latitude. Once these references have been secured, birth times must be converted to Greenwich Mean Time (GMT), degree compensations made, and hour corrections undertaken either from noon or midnight. It is a complicated process that most astrologers now eschew.

To use this book effectively and to abet your curiosity and enthusiasm to create, review, and understand any natal chart with ease and convenience, you can get a chart calculated quickly—and free—online. Simply enter any date, hour, country, and city of birth and a birth chart—along with a grid of aspects and transits, if also requested—will appear in seconds. Be aware that the more accurate the data, the more accurate the chart. (Suggested websites, software, and other resources can be found in the resources section of this book.)

THE KEY TO AN ACCURATE BIRTH CHART

To create an accurate birth chart, regardless of how the chart is developed or obtained, first and foremost, you will need to know your date, time, and place of birth. If you don't know your time of birth, check your original birth certificate. If you don't have your original birth certificate, contact the Bureau of Records (or Vital Statistics) in your city and obtain a copy. Some bureaus refer to these certificates as "vault" copies because birth certificates are now computer-generated and do not contain this information. The original document is kept in a vault, and for an additional fee, you can usually request a certified photocopy of the original certificate and have it mailed to you.

You might also contact the hospital in which you were born. Some hospitals will accommodate your request; others will not.

If neither of these methods works, ask your parents, grandparents, or other close relatives or family friends. Even if you don't discover an exact birth time, you should come away with a good estimate. If all else fails, use 6:00 a.m. as your time of birth. Even without knowing your time of birth, you will be able to get a relatively accurate indication of which signs your planets were placed in, even if you are unable to determine house placements or your ascendant.

READING A BIRTH CHART

If you have a birth chart constructed by a professional or computer, it will look somewhat like the following:

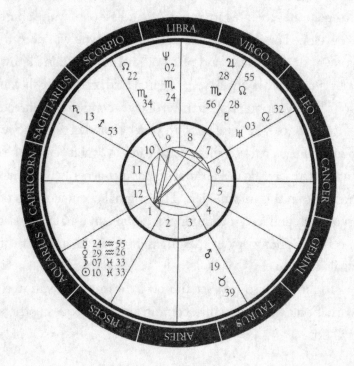

At first glance, you'll see a wheel filled with unfamiliar symbols and numbers. Making sense of this is easier than you think.

In addition to wheels, many computer programs also print out tables that display this information more clearly. Placing the information in a table makes it easier to understand and interpret, as shown with information taken from the wheel:

PLANET	GLYPH	SIGN	DEGREES	HOUSE
Sun	☉	Pisces	10 ♓ 33	1
Moon	☽	Pisces	07 ♓ 33	1
Mercury	☿	Aquarius	24 ♒ 55	1
Venus	♀	Aquarius	29 ♒ 24	1
Mars	♂	Taurus	19 ♉ 39	3
Jupiter	♃	Virgo	28 ♍ 56	8
Saturn	♄	Sagittarius	13 ♐ 53	10
Uranus	♅	Leo	28 ♌ 55	7
Neptune	♆	Scorpio	02 ♏ 24	9
Pluto	♇	Leo	28 ♌ 55	7
North Node	☊	Scorpio	22 ♏ 34	10
Ascendant	ASC	Capricorn	29 ♑ 26	1

It helps to familiarize yourself with the various glyphs used as a shorthand for the signs and planets. In this example, the configuration of the Sun at 10 ♓ 33 means 10 degrees, 33 minutes of Pisces.

Once you have all your planets in their signs and houses placed in a chart or table, you can easily look up the information in the following chapters to read the interpretations given.

Many computer-generated charts provide an aspect grid. This is a chart that displays the aspects or notable angles that various planets make to one another in a birth chart.

Aspects

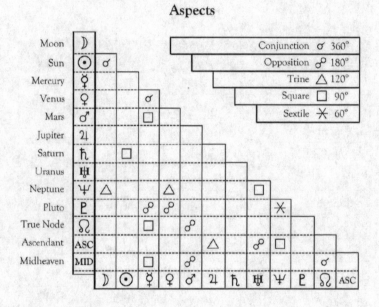

Moon	☽											
Sun	☉	☌										
Mercury	☿											
Venus	♀			☌								
Mars	♂			□								
Jupiter	♃											
Saturn	♄		□									
Uranus	♅											
Neptune	♆	△		△			□					
Pluto	♇		☍	☍				✳				
True Node	☊		□		☍							
Ascendant	ASC			△		☍	□					
Midheaven	MID		□		☍					☌		
		☽	☉	☿	♀	♂	♃	♄	♅	♆	♇	☊	ASC

Conjunction ☌ 360°
Opposition ☍ 180°
Trine △ 120°
Square □ 90°
Sextile ✳ 60°

Explanations and interpretations of aspects are covered in chapter 7.

HOW TO USE THIS BOOK

The quickest and easiest way to get a first glimpse at your horoscope is to save and print out your birth chart, along with any additional charts and information provided regarding the houses and aspects. Once you have that, you can begin reading the explanations of your Sun Sign and its traits, along with the placements of all your other planets in their signs and houses, your rising sign/ascendant, and so on. The combination of these descriptions will provide you with a personalized portrait of your personality and potential. From there, you can create charts of friends, partners, and family members and gain insight into their personality traits, too.

INTERPRETATION

The three major factors to look at when interpreting a chart are planets, signs, and houses. Planets represent energies or "what," signs represent "how" the planets operate, and houses represent the environment or "where."

Whether you are interpreting your natal chart or that of a family member or friend, start with a broad perspective. Add up the number of planets you have in both masculine and feminine signs to see if they lean active or passive. How many cardinal, fixed, and mutable planets appear in the chart? Categorize the planets by their elements and see which ones dominate. Does the chart lack fire? Air? Earth? Water? Are the planets mostly emotional, intellectual, or theoretical, or are they balanced? These are some of the first attributes worth examining to get an overview of the unique traits in anyone's chart.

Exploring all the characteristics and potentials in your chart is interesting, informative, and fun. As you begin your study of astrology and chart interpretation, you might find that certain traits show up repeatedly, while others contradict each other. Keep in mind that sometimes you might read something about yourself that is dead-on while, other times, you might not readily relate to such a trait. The entire process should be taken as a whole. Every person has a blend of positive and negative traits, qualities that are dynamic, and qualities that are understated or subliminal. There are almost always bright sides and dark sides, things that come easily, and things that present challenges. As you pursue the path to self-awareness, you will become more open-minded about what you discover. Sometimes the things we learn that make us uncomfortable are the very things that eventually help us grow. An affliction or hard aspect in a chart is a chance for understanding, overcoming obstacles, and, ultimately, greater personal development.

4

The Sun Signs

The twelve signs of the Zodiac comprise the zodiacal belt, which is the backdrop by which we identify Earth's transit. We are geocentric, which means that our astrological orientation stems from our perspective of the planets from our view on Earth. As Earth transits through its elliptical course, it will move through a different sign each month. These "Sun" Signs are consistent—the same Sun Sign appears at the same time each year. It takes Earth twelve months to complete its rotation as it passes through each of the twelve Sun Signs.

Early in the development of man, he recognized the warmth, light, and energy he received from the Sun. Like the Sun itself, the Sun Sign is the most vital, energetic, and powerful part of a natal chart. It determines your position in life—your outlook, success, progress, and, most importantly, how you come to know yourself.

In psychological terms, the Sun Sign represents the unconscious part of your psyche that moves you toward fulfilling of your inherent needs. The Sun Sign contains your entire survival kit—how you relate, project, and respond to others and the world at large.

There are no good or bad Sun Signs; each has a unique set of positive and negative qualities. The Sun Sign is your chosen destiny. It reflects your personal spirit and will, and you are born to use it. It is something you cannot avoid but, instead, must understand and work through.

The Sun, in combination with your Moon and ascendant, defines the qualities of your personality in this chosen lifetime, but only the Sun carries your destiny—the other planets are actors in supporting roles.

Each Sun Sign is also divided into three ten-degree sections called *decans*. A decan adds a personality edge, like a flavor, to a sequence of dates within each Sun Sign. The first decan of any sign spans zero to ten degrees; the second decan is ten to twenty degrees; the third decan is twenty to thirty degrees. Each decan is characterized by one of three planets that share the same element of your birth sign, depending on where the Sun was positioned at the time of your birth.

Depending on the year of your birth, the dates when the Sun enters each sign may differ by one day, so a well-calculated and constructed natal chart is necessary to ensure exact Sun Sign dates for any year.

Please note: The Sun Sign descriptions reflect each sign's astrological gender (i.e., masculine or feminine polarity). In addition, the dates listed for each sign can change by one day, depending on the year. For accuracy, consult your personal birth chart.

ARIES (MARCH 21–APRIL 19)

Symbol—The Ram
Ruling Planet—Mars
Element—Fire
Cross—Cardinal
Group—Emotional
Gender—Masculine
House Ruled—First
Famous Arians—Lady Gaga, Elton John, Vincent van Gogh, Thomas Jefferson, Tennessee Williams, Reese Witherspoon, Harry Houdini, Leonardo da Vinci, Eric Clapton, Maya Angelou

Basic Personality

Aries, the first sign of the Zodiac, represents the beginning. He is generous, moral, and has physical courage, which, given to him by his ruling planet of Mars, endows him with physical strength and stamina. Aries can be highly intellectual and innovative, direct, and forceful.

Aries is an initiator. He likes to get going, he likes to *do*—but that never guarantees that he will finish. He needs lots of praise and encouragement to keep going. Without this, he becomes anxiety-ridden and prone to failure.

Inside of Aries lurks an insecurity, a sense of inadequacy that often leads to extravagance, jealousy, or arrogance. The result is disappointment and disillusionment. When Aries is troubled in this way, his physical courage, forcefulness, and directness become compulsive, even impulsive, as he gives little thought to his actions.

The urge to move is utmost to Aries, but he needs to learn to stand still, stop, and consider if there is a reason to move. Since Aries is naturally fast, quick, and alert, he finds it hard to control his impulsiveness—as soon as a thought is in his brain, it's out of his mouth. He'll jump into the water and then realize he can't swim. He means well, but when things backfire, he gets anxious. If he holds back or tries to reconcile his impulses, he starts to feel guilty and then winds up in a bad funk.

Aries has an innate fear of rejection, which he often uses as a defense mechanism—he rejects for fear that he might be rejected. If he does not overcome this problem or receive positive stroking with the genuine care and love he requires, he will feel incomplete.

Aries desires success, and if he is not successful, it is usually of his own doing. He lacks a sense of proportion. He becomes overly optimistic, extravagant, or makes well-intended but grandiose claims that he cannot always back up. Should his expectations not be met, emotional problems ensue.

Aries is youthful, and since, astrologically, he is a beginner, he is often naive, lacks insight, and is unable to correctly assess human nature. He needs to develop self-awareness, which is something that takes maturity, education, and reinforcement. His instability—this itch that makes him go from one thing to the next—can, with the development of self-awareness, make him more consistent, allowing him to bring ideas and projects to completion and, ultimately, achieve.

Overall, Aries is mainly strong, formidable, and successful. If he overcomes the fear of rejection and becomes secure in his actions and accomplishments, he will meet his ultimate objectives and destiny head-on.

Talents and Abilities

Aries constantly expresses himself, so journalism is an excellent field of endeavor. As a journalist, he can actualize self-expression through travel, excitement, and "on the go" experiences. TV, radio, and theater can also safely provide Aries with outlets for the flights of fantasy to which he is heir. These are all good career fields that allow for change and little boredom.

Since Mars rules this sign and, mythologically, Mars is the ancient god of war, it makes Aries very much at home in any career in the military. Unless he has a strong disciplinarian influence, Aries is not likely to be self-disciplined. The military provides discipline, structure, and danger. It is a career field that will allow Aries to express his courage and inner "knight in shining armor" qualities.

Health and Physical Traits

Aries rules the head, spinal cord, sensory nerves, face, and lower jaw. Frequently, Aries has scars on his face.

Aries is also prone to nervous tension and anxiety.

When Aries is ridden with guilt, in extreme cases, it can produce impotence in the male and frigidity in the female.

Family Relationships

Aries is a masculine / father-dominated sign, which means he has issues to work out with his father. The relationship between the Aries child and his father is basically one of fear. Whether good or bad, the father is more than likely going to be aggressive and manifest the very quality that Aries needs to curb. Bearing the rest of the chart, he will have either an isolated/uncommunicative or aggressive/authoritative dad. He will imitate his father's behavior while copying his mother's emotional structure. If there is parental tension in the household, Aries starts feeling guilty and assumes that he's responsible for the rift. At that point, he tries his best to reconcile Mom and Dad. His needs turn egocentric and create selfishness.

The Aries child is an aggressive daredevil who will take his parents to task. He's always moving and doesn't hold still. It is best to give this child free rein but with guidance. Guidance is a means to get this child to think—he acts before he thinks and expects to find results after the action. It is nearly impossible to get him to understand the concept of consequences. The Aries child often winds up with scars and bruises because he is a born risk-taker. He must not be contained, but instead, learn how to contain himself. Enrolling the Aries child in a martial arts class or some other structured activity or sport will help channel his energy.

Partnerships

When relating to others, Aries is usually aggressive, talkative, and pushy—whether he's selling himself or projecting his fears. He can't control himself—he is "on" all the time and can be an extremely tiring partner. He is sexual, forceful, and spontaneous. Partnerships are difficult for Aries because he is innately afraid of rejection. Aries translates anything that resists his desires or isn't conducted when or how he wants it as rejection. If this happens too often, jealousy is aroused. He can ram the walls or get sexually overwrought. He is insecure and slow to mature. Feelings must be explained to him. As a partner, it is recommended that you be gentle, soothing, and able to accept this often immature sign. As Aries matures, however, he acquires sophistication, and therefore his rougher qualities begin to subside. He'll be a far better partner later in life—particularly after he passes midlife. At that point, his intelligence and accomplishments can show through.

DECANS

FIRST DECAN: **Aries/Aries**—(0 to 10 degrees or approximately March 21–30)

This decan is doubly ruled by Mars so that Aries's Martian quality is very evident in this placement. The inability to think before expressing himself creates difficulty for this decan. Aries/Aries is talkative; he moves around but is not conscious of the impact his indiscreet talk or actions have on someone else. He has little insight into other people. Since he acts without thinking, he's prone to repeat his mistakes again and again, always wondering why he elicits strange and adverse reactions from others.

SECOND DECAN: **Aries/Leo**—(10 to 20 degrees or approximately March 31–April 9)

In this decan, the influences of Leo and the Sun are going to tone down the native characteristics of Aries. He is going to be less self-centered and more "we" oriented. His ambitions are directed, and he has a flair for drama and passion, which Leo amply provides. Aries/Leo is intense and emotional and needs lightening up. He has a low tolerance for pain and always thinks his pain is worse than everyone else's.

THIRD DECAN: **Aries/Sagittarius**—(20 to 30 degrees or approximately April 10–19)

Jupiter's influence on Sagittarius is going to give this decan of Aries a whole different attitude. He is going to be far more outgoing and philosophical. He might be more physical and have well-disciplined energy, which can be favorably applied to sports and outdoor activities, as well as philosophical interests. This is the most restless of the decans because that Jupiter quality that expands him will also keep him moving and focused.

TAURUS (APRIL 20–MAY 20)

Symbol—The Bull
Ruling Planet—Venus

Element—Earth
Cross—Fixed
Group—Emotional
Gender—Feminine
House Ruled—Second
Famous Taureans—Barbra Streisand, Adolf Hitler, Sigmund
Freud, William Shakespeare, Dwayne "The Rock" Johnson,
Adele, Salvador Dalí, Queen Elizabeth II, George Clooney,
Jerry Seinfeld

Basic Personality

Taurus, the second sign of the Zodiac, is conservative, a
meticulous planner, and an incredibly artistic individual.
Taurus is honest and childlike. She is consistent, dependable, basically selfless, and generous. She has enormous
willpower, is self-disciplined, and tenacious.

Taurus has the power of the body. Because her physical
structure is muscular and robust, Taurus can simply give and
then quickly regenerate. She possesses healing abilities that
can provide great comfort to others.

A very sexual sign, Taurus is tuned in to the sensual needs
of herself and her partners. The five senses—hearing, smell,
taste, touch, and sight—are keen and well developed. Only
an old or sick Taurus loses the use of her senses.

Taurus tends to derive security from the material, so she
begins to amass. Possessions compensate for whatever she
feels is lacking in herself and her life and help lower anxieties about these insecurities.

Personality contradictions set in when there are negative afflictions for Taurus. This so-called conservative, meticulous planner can suddenly become a rigid, stubborn, selfish, and self-restricting individual. She might give you blind devotion, but you can be sure she expects it in return. If it is not obtained, she becomes hostile, resentful, suspicious, oversensitive, and hot-tempered.

Loyalty is utmost to Taurus; she is loyal and will test others' devotion. She loses her loyalty only as a result of having her ego attacked or being lied to—and if you lie to a Taurus, she will more than likely never trust you again.

Taurus automatically holds back and represses emotions and aggressions beyond the call of duty. Taurus wants to let go and move forward but is afraid that such actions might be considered unacceptable. Since Taurus is ruled by the refined and feminine planet of Venus, it makes her self-conscious and embarrassed by anything that is "gross." These suppressions often wind up producing overindulgences and excesses of all kinds—food, drink, sex . . . you name it.

Taurus also exhibits a morbid dread of change. Since it is a fixed sign, the native finds it difficult to alter her emotions. She might change concepts or ideas, but emotions stay bottled up. This makes her a master at holding grudges. Taurus takes it and takes it until she cannot take it anymore, and then, watch out—like a charging bull, she will simply explode and take you right over the hill with her. At that point, Taurus can throw tantrums like a baby whose outbursts can be triggered by the slightest thing, and she will care little about them.

To cope or to overcome old wounds, Taurus must find a more productive method of release. She must learn to keep her emotions, temper, and innate stubbornness in balance. Most importantly, she must learn how to forgive.

Taurus bases her security on knowing. Education and the enlargement of thought are vital to Taurus since she rules the second house, which represents the possession of concepts and the ability (or inability) to act on them.

Taurus reaches maturity somewhere in midlife, usually over the age of forty. About that time, she becomes more knowledgeable and stable—someone who will most likely have a long life and a youthful personality. If Taurus learns to understand and control her temper, she can work well under pressure, be creative and talented, capable, and extraordinarily productive.

Talents and Abilities
Since Venus rules the throat, Taurus usually possesses a beautiful speaking or singing voice—Barbra Streisand and Adele were both born under the sign of Taurus.

The influence of Venus produces an artistic ability and appreciation that makes Taurus a successful artist or writer.

Taurus is also adept at handling money. She understands stocks and commodities and can make an excellent financier or accountant.

Since Taurus both amasses and preserves, she can be successful in restoration, renovation, and antiques.

Love of beautiful things allows Taurus to thrive as a clothing designer, makeup artist, perfumer, or jeweler.

Health and Physical Traits

Taurus rules the thyroid gland and the throat. Because Venus rules Taurus, it also rules the bloodstream and the sugar level in the pancreas.

Taurus needs a lot of exercise. She won't do it voluntarily and really must be prodded into getting physical. Aerobics can be beneficial by helping Taurus sweat, expand the lungs, and clear the bloodstream. Blood needs to clear itself of carbon, which Taurus retains and which slows her down, makes her tired, and turns her into a couch potato. Take heed, Taurus: It's time to get moving!

Family Relationships

Taurus is a feminine / mother-dominated sign, so she's very much a reflection of her mother. Until she matures, she winds up emulating Mother. Since her mother is usually strict and demanding, Taurus must avoid becoming overbearing and imposing her concepts and ideas on others, whether family, friends, or associates. As a result of having a strong mother, many Taurus males fear that women have much too much power. This can create power struggles or simply become threatening to relationships.

As a parent, Taurus shines at handling babies, possessing a natural healing and soothing quality that is wonderful and nurturing to infants and children. The clashes usually start when children are older and begin having ideas of their own. That's the time Taurus must learn to let go.

The Taurus mother has a personal need to keep her children the cleanest and the smartest. She is loving and means well, but she projects her sense of refinement onto her children, wanting them to be the best. If she bears a child with a less cooperative Sun Sign, clashes will result, and the Taurus mother will get hurt. She doesn't understand that the most important thing she can do is take her energy back and stop projecting herself onto her children. She must learn to look for her own identity and desires, go out and do her own thing, and get off her children's backs so that they can be true to themselves.

A Taurus dad is a nice, indulgent guy. He's placid and usually goes along with Mom—he's a "good guy" and nurturing. Both Taurus parents are generous, love their children, and will indulge them.

Partnerships

Overall, Taurus males and females make good partners. One of the difficulties a Taurus female has is that she projects her energy onto her husband. She is motherly and loving, sometimes to the point of smothering. She tends to be jealous and possessive.

The Taurus male wants adulation and recognition,

particularly from his family. He is a good provider and needs his family to show appreciation for his efforts.

DECANS

FIRST DECAN: **Taurus/Taurus**—(0 to 10 degrees or approximately April 20–30)

In this decan, Taurus can be stubborn and bullish; she will push rather than move gently. She is sexually oriented but predominantly sensual. Earth/Venus requires indulgence and pleasure, and Taurus will frequently indulge in food to sublimate what is lacking in other areas of her life. She resists emotional and psychological pain beyond the call of duty and can withstand anything. She can also be benevolent.

SECOND DECAN: **Taurus/Virgo**—(10 to 20 degrees or approximately May 1–10)

This Virgo/Mercury influence makes for a more intellectual Taurus. She is prone to think rather than act or respond. In this decan, Taurus doesn't want the contamination of others' input—she needs to get the answers by herself. If afflicted, she might be unadaptable or unsociable.

THIRD DECAN: **Taurus/Capricorn**—(20 to 30 degrees or approximately May 11–20)

Capricorn/Saturn influences this decan, and Saturn is restrictive, making Taurus more materialistic. If afflicted, there can be a fear of deprivation, so Taurus must trust in her abilities to make money or else she will wind up becoming stingy, pessimistic, conventional, and unwilling to take a chance. This decan needs to develop faith and seriously consider the concept that hard work and mastery can result in rewards.

GEMINI (MAY 21-JUNE 20)

Symbol—The Twins
Ruling Planet—Mercury
Element—Air
Cross—Mutable
Group—Emotional
Gender—Masculine
House Ruled—Third
Famous Geminis—John F. Kennedy, Marilyn Monroe, Paul McCartney, Anne Frank, Bob Dylan, Queen Victoria, Clint Eastwood, Judy Garland, Donald Trump, Tupac Shakur

Basic Personality

Gemini, ruled by Mercury, is heady and intelligent, possessing lightning quickness of the mind. He is witty and articulate with a natural sense of comic timing. He is also an experience seeker, versatile, and adaptable.

Like all air signs, Gemini is a sign of extremes. He is also a double sign—the sign of the twins. This duality gives him both manual and mental dexterity but also makes him inconsistent, superficial, irritable, and even irritating. He can become obsessive, compulsive, and excessively analytical about anything and everything.

Gemini is naturally nosy. He desires to know about others but, ironically, reveals little of himself. If afflicted, he can become emotionally dependent, which, in turn, spurs hostility—this is a person who can bite the hand that feeds him.

If negatively afflicted, Gemini's natural glibness and wit become distorted, making him a liar and a cheat. He has a cunning command of words and will verbally cut down his foes. At his worst, he can be cold-blooded and cynical with an "I don't care" attitude. This is one of the cruelest aspects of this personality—he can reach a point where he truly doesn't give a damn.

Gemini often feels inadequate, and that can make him hostile and adversarial. He'll argue and fight in an opposing manner—when you become emotional, he becomes intellectual; when you're cool, calm, and rational, he becomes overemotional. Whenever Gemini gets too overwhelmed or feels that he's not going to win, he will simply disappear. It takes a long time before Gemini learns to control the inconsistency in his nature. That's why he is often referred to as "a butterfly."

There is a constant striving for balance between mind and emotion within Gemini. He works to keep his logic and feelings on an even keel even if he ultimately winds up creating chaos around him.

To keep healthy and productive, Gemini must eventually accept the duality of his nature, which can be accomplished through education. When his intellect is enhanced and self-knowledge gained, Gemini becomes a sophisticated, adaptable, and easygoing individual—a delight, who is mentally stimulating and can think on his feet. When he becomes unrepressed, he will operate well under pressure, be free of anxiety, and able to control his innate propensity toward overanalyzing himself and others.

Talents and Abilities

As a master of words, Gemini thrives as a writer or an actor, particularly in the theater. In acting, that butterfly quality is an advantage—Gemini can go from one role to another and get out of himself through his command of words. His innate sense of the ridiculous makes Gemini a good comedian, too.

Gemini possesses dexterity in the hands, arms, legs, and feet and can be a good dancer. He is also successful in any form of sales.

Health and Physical Traits

Gemini rules the lungs, all fiber tissue, and the shoulders down to the hands.

Gemini tends to be lean unless afflicted. Because he's mutable, he should take care of his central nervous system and periodically rest. He has a predisposition to nervousness and allergies and must watch his diet. His emotional swings from logical to emotional may make him prone to bipolar disorder and, in highly afflicted cases, schizophrenia.

Gemini must be careful, particularly if there is a Sagittarius aspect in his chart, of airborne and food-related allergies, which, if left untreated, can produce asthma. Gemini rules the lungs, so expansion of the lungs through swimming, dancing, or similar pursuits is vital to him. He should take care of his lungs or else run the risk of winding up with respiratory problems like emphysema.

Family Relationships

Gemini is usually raised in a household where his mother and father are talkers. They don't touch each other, so Gemini isn't privy to displays of physical affection. Everything that goes on in his household is so verbal that Gemini learns that if he wants attention, he is simply going to have to contradict everyone—it's the only way he will succeed at getting noticed. If he is not conscious of this action, he's going to spend the rest of his life contradicting situations and people solely for the sake of being heard. This will only result in his own unhappy and unhealthy isolation.

The Gemini child is attractive, talkative, and friendly. He is also restless, active, and nosy. It's hard to get his attention and even harder to keep it. He needs to learn to calm down. He needs sleep and proper nutrition. He doesn't like restriction, so he will disassociate or create chaos to get attention or get his own way. The Gemini child needs mental challenges and discipline to keep going—he needs to learn mastery. You can't punish a Gemini child, but you can discipline him by arousing his interest and curiosity, helping him finish what he starts, and remaining consistent.

The Gemini parent is confusing and inconsistent, lacking

the ability to provide personal attention. Though the Gemini parent cares about his child and the child's education, he often winds up getting more involved with the political issues of the school than the educational needs of his child.

Partnerships

Partnerships are difficult for Gemini because he requires constant stimulation. He is easily bored, dislikes familiarity, and is always looking for change, particularly in his youth. He can be superficial in both his personal relationships and business partnerships since he doesn't always hold up his end of the bargain.

In marriage, Geminis need to roam, which creates loneliness for their partners. They are not often dependable and are usually not great earners until later in life. If you're in love with a Gemini, you will have to put up with a lot and identify your role in the relationship. The best approach is to take Gemini with a grain of salt and not be possessive—he's really not dangerous and will always come back home.

DECANS

FIRST DECAN: **Gemini/Gemini**—(0 to 10 degrees or approximately May 21–30)

Gemini's Mercury rulership is strong in this decan, emphasizing that unstable, butterfly quality—talkative, babbling, but not necessarily cohesive. He will also play that mental game where when you're intellectual, he's emotional, and vice versa.

The first decan of Gemini is indiscreet. He'll open his mouth and say things that are childlike but often hurtful.

SECOND DECAN: **Gemini/Libra**—(10 to 20 degrees or approximately May 31–June 10)

Gemini, in this decan, flavored by Libra/Venus, is artistic and has a creative flair. This Venus/Mercury combination creates a gentle, likable, and nonconfrontational Gemini. If afflicted, however, Gemini/Libra can be mentally and physically lazy, which can lead to restlessness. He will lack discipline, start but never finish, and ultimately prevent his artistic expression from blossoming.

THIRD DECAN: **Gemini/Aquarius**—(20 to 30 degrees or approximately June 11–20)

This decan has the influence of Aquarius/Uranus, which, combined with Gemini, is excellent. It makes this Gemini quick-minded and prophetic. He can think beyond the present and instinctively know where the next business trend is heading and go straight for it. Gemini, in this decan, has an enormous ability for success in business, especially in science, medicine, big corporations, and group settings.

CANCER (JUNE 21–JULY 22)

Symbol—The Crab
Ruling Planet—Moon

Element—Water

Cross—Cardinal

Group—Emotional

Gender—Feminine

House Ruled—Fourth

Famous Cancerians—Princess Diana, Julius Caesar, Tom Hanks, Elon Musk, Ernest Hemingway, Ringo Starr, Rembrandt, Henry VIII, Meryl Streep, Tom Cruise

Basic Personality

Those born under the sign of Cancer are referred to as Moon children because they are vulnerable to the changing phases of the Moon, the ruling planet of Cancer.

Cancer is sensitive, shy, and retiring by nature. She can understand and feel for others in a psychic manner. Cancer is imaginative, dependable, conservative, and incredibly loving. She has a great need to be loved, which can, in turn, lead to many disappointments of the heart.

Cancer is a family- and home-oriented individual, and this extends to the workplace, town, country, or even the universal family. At any club, office, or community gathering, you'll find that it's usually Cancer who supplies the food—she makes sure there is coffee and cake and whatever else is necessary to secure the comfort of the group.

Cancer is inherently moody due to the waxing and waning of the Moon. If you're having trouble with a Cancer, wait two days . . . the Moon phases will alter, and so will she.

When Cancer is negatively afflicted, she becomes touchy.

Instead of being sensitive, she's prickly; instead of being shy, she's hostile. This ability to ensure that everyone has a cup of coffee and a piece of cake can transform into stinginess. She becomes spiteful, hardened, and literally as tight as a crab's ass.

Part of Cancer's internal conflict is that she feels and senses but doesn't necessarily interpret correctly—she misconstrues and personalizes things. If Cancer doesn't learn to catch herself doing this and discipline herself, she will become increasingly angry, hostile, and, eventually, paranoid.

By nature, Cancer is a collector and a hoarder. Unlike Taurus, whose propensity for collecting comes from a Venus-ruled desire for beauty and security, Cancer hoards out of self-stroking, self-caring, and possessiveness. Because Cancer usually has a difficult emotional life, which is common to all water signs, the deprivation of emotion and occasional bouts of self-pity make her possessive and hungry to hold on to everything. And it is truly a "hunger." No matter how successful, Cancer always harbors a need to be stroked and loved. Even when she receives it, she doesn't always recognize or believe it. Within Cancer is a void that exists from the moment she is born because Cancer/Capricorn is the "polarity of starvation." This means that in a past-life experience, she more than likely starved. As a result, Cancer takes this unconscious physical starvation and brings it into this life as emotional starvation.

The physical and psychological strength or weakness of

a Cancer Sun Sign is determined by the the Moon's place-ment in the birth chart.

It is interesting to note that the United States became a nation under Cancer—July 4, 1776—and the United States has become the caretaker of the world. The heart of this country, like Cancer itself, is selfless and shares its abundance.

Talents and Abilities

Because of her emotional personality, Cancer makes a wonderful actor. In the world of business, she can be an excellent financier. Her keen intuition and all-consuming need for security make the world of finance a wonderful and comfortable place for Cancer. There are many wealthy Cancerians. Once Cancer feels secure and achieves, she also becomes philanthropic.

The attic or closet of any Cancer, a collector by nature, will likely be filled with many interesting and valuable things—antiques, baseball cards, comic books, coins, memorabilia—that can be turned into a serious hobby or side business for profit.

With her inherent fear of starvation, you can also find Cancer involved with food as a restaurateur, chef, or caterer.

Health and Physical Traits

Cancer rules the breasts, stomach, spleen, and all elastic tis-sue. For Cancer, one of the difficulties of her life is going to be illness. The Cancer child usually suffers from many psychosomatic illnesses—her innate and acute emotional sensitivity and inconsistency leave her physically vulnerable and "lacking."

Cancer is prone to digestive problems. Since she is afraid of starvation, she sometimes lacks digestive enzymes and can't process food completely or make proper use of nutrients internally. This can be resolved by dietary changes and improved eating habits. Overeating or eating disorders are quite typical of this sign. Cancer frequently nurtures herself through food.

Calcium shortages during maturation can create pregnancy problems. Cancer women are often unable to conceive or are prone to miscarriages. It is helpful for Cancer women to supplement their diets with calcium and to get lots of exercise—they tend to be couch potatoes.

Family Relationships

Cancer is a mother-dominated sign, so she spends her life copying Mom. Depending on the placement of the Moon within the chart, this could be a love/hate relationship.

Cancer has trouble keeping her relationships with her parents in balance. Her emotional inconsistency keeps her bouncing back and forth between the two so that she can wind up playing a risky game of dividing Mom and Dad to conquer each separately and, ultimately, wind up achieving nothing.

The Cancer child is sensitive and picks up the emotional vibes in her household. Since she is also easily hurt, she often withdraws, feeling deprived and sorry for herself. She is basically shy but will always find a way to get what she needs. The Cancer child knows how to press the buttons of concern in others and is quick to complain.

As a parent, Cancer is possessive. The Cancer mother worries about her baby before it is born. Since she usually battles health problems and illnesses throughout her life, she often carries forth this concern and projects it on her children.

Partnerships

Cancer is romantic. The Cancer male does not go looking for sex. Falling in love is the highest priority for both men and women.

The Cancer male is in a relationship for the long haul. He enjoys romance and intimacy until his last breath. In the female, Cancer deems sex important for childbearing only and often turns away from her husband sexually early in the marriage. She is quite content being a housewife. For her, cleaning a window is more satisfying than a romp in bed. She becomes involved with the mechanics of family life and designates roles to each family member—Dad is the provider, she is the caretaker, and so on. The Cancer female frequently gets into trouble because she exaggerates her emotional/physical weaknesses. Instead of being tired, she's sick; instead of saying something doesn't appeal to her, she gets a headache. She has a cop-out for everything.

If afflicted, Cancer can go from being romantic to being

so domineering, tyrannical, and self-centered that it leaves little room for anyone else's ideas or feelings.

DECANS

FIRST DECAN: **Cancer/Cancer**—(0 to 10 degrees or approximately June 21–July 1)

The Moon's influence results in an instability that can lead to unnecessary sensitivity and self-pity. Spite often grips this decan. Cancer needs to learn how to control her emotional responses.

Water holds within it a primordial longing that is hard to define. It is a desire to return to the womb—Cancer wants comfort and has a longing to be protected and nurtured by a parent or spouse.

SECOND DECAN: **Cancer/Scorpio**—(10 to 20 degrees or approximately July 2–12)

The Scorpio/Pluto influence leads to some strong and powerful qualities. This Cancer can be psychic and make an excellent medium because she will have the ability to receive information from another source other than her ego. This is usually a wonderful and sensitive Cancer. If afflicted, however, she can be stubborn, domineering, jealous, and vindictive.

THIRD DECAN: **Cancer/Pisces**—(20 to 30 degrees or approximately July 13–22)

With the flavor of Pisces, Cancer will be sympathetic and able to absorb emotions and empathize. This is the most psychic of all the Cancer decans because perceptions about people and things will be sharp. If badly aspected, however, this can switch to a form of martyrdom—someone who serves beyond the call of duty and can lose herself in an idealistic world-savior concept. She can become completely self-sacrificing toward a person, cause, or ideal, especially if it entails influencing the masses.

LEO (JULY 23–AUGUST 22)

Symbol—The Lion
Ruling Planet—Sun
Element—Fire
Cross—Fixed
Group—Intellectual
Gender—Masculine
House Ruled—Fifth
Famous Leos—Jacqueline Kennedy Onassis, Mick Jagger, Carl Jung, Viola Davis, Napoleon, J. K. Rowling, Jennifer Lopez, Andy Warhol, Madonna, George Bernard Shaw

Basic Personality

Leo epitomizes the classic sense of masculinity. He represents energy and vital forces at the highest level. Leo is generous, loyal, dramatic, and outgoing—this is a sunny disposition in the truest sense of the word. The Sun rules Leo, and like the Sun, he positively shines.

Leo is masterful and dynamic, self-aware, and self-assured. Like an actor walking onto a stage and knowing every line and every spot where he needs to stand, he commands that stage as if he owns it. He radiates strength and courage and possesses a high threshold for pain and adversity—there is little he cannot withstand.

Leo has an enormous drive and a desire to succeed—he has the gift of leadership. He is a born leader who can motivate any group toward success. He possesses a natural flair for inspiring others to think and act.

Fire signs, in general, are particularly intelligent; all they need is honing, polishing, and education. If Leo can go from acquiring information to applying it, he will invariably find success and, most importantly, develop wisdom.

Leo unintentionally draws envy from others. Even the most uneducated or unpolished Leo has a regal quality and a commanding gait to his walk. In the Leo male, the fashion in which he carries his body makes others feel attracted to yet threatened by him. In the female, it's a charisma, a self-assuredness that others tend to envy. These majestic, confident qualities are so unconscious to Leo that he needs to learn to curb them; otherwise, they can wind up becoming a disguise for doubt. Even with all his self-confidence, Leo has a seed of doubt about himself. If that doubt takes hold and becomes more prominent than his positive qualities, his ego will start requiring constant reassurance.

If afflicted, Leo's majestic personality becomes proud,

and pride often becomes blinding and dangerous. Leo is a poor judge of character and can easily be taken in by others. The greatest traumas are suffered by Leo, whether a Leo Sun, Moon, or ascendant. Leo is the "sign of victimization." He is overly sensitive to other people's needs. He has an overwhelming desire to please, which leads to the denial of his own needs so that someone else can benefit. This is what is meant by *victimization*. Leo is proud of his intelligence and needs to prove how smart he is. Assets can become liabilities when misused or abused.

Since Leo isn't a good judge of people, he is susceptible to flattery, which becomes his greatest undoing—it makes him arrogant, overbearing, and blustery.

Leo has an overwhelming desire to please. This desire often leads to a denial of his own needs and energies. It can make him too easygoing and lazy, like a fat cat on a windowsill. When you prod or demand something from Leo, he responds like a firecracker—he explodes with a quick, bad temper. Deep in his heart, Leo knows he must move, but since he's always trying to please everybody, he winds up holding himself back or denying the self entirely. This creates depression because his seed of self-doubt becomes self-defeating.

When Leo recognizes and values his self-worth, his pride will no longer be a source of self-victimization; he will be strong and secure—a shining light to himself and those around him.

Talents and Abilities

There is nothing finer than a Leo actor. He can thoroughly transform himself into any character or situation.

Radio or television announcing is perfect for the Leo male—the resonance in his voice is unmistakable. Even as a baby, he sounds like a little foghorn. (Leo females have voices that aren't as melodic and are almost squeaky.)

The Leo female has unquestionable intelligence and needs mental stimulation. With her keen retention of facts, she makes a good accountant, people manager, or office manager. She needs to succeed. She loves big challenges and multifaceted responsibilities.

Health and Physical Traits

Leo rules the heart, which is the central pump of the body, mind, and soul universe.

Leo is strong and usually muscular. Both the male and female have a body structure that makes them powerful—a power that emanates from the level of the aura.

Leo has good posture, a smooth gait, and, like a lion, he is ready to pounce at every turn. The hair of Leo is unmistakable—abundant, thick, and beautiful.

Family Relationships

As a father-dominated sign, the Leo male has issues to resolve with his father. He is afraid of being rejected by him, so he elevates his father to a level of which he might not always be deserving. Leo also develops a sense of competitiveness with his father to feel and identify with his own masculinity. The Leo female identifies with her father, too—she needs his strength and attention.

Interestingly, Leo himself makes a wonderful father. He is that rare bird who will often stay in a deteriorating marriage for the sake of his children. His intense relationship with his own father makes him protective and fearful of losing his children.

The Leo female makes a good mother, too. She is strong and supportive of her family. However, she should be careful not to be authoritative—she thinks she knows better and can be argumentative and demanding. She sets standards that are predicated on her opinions and ego with little insight into the talents and limitations of her children. The Leo mother sees her children as a reflection of herself. Her intentions are good but often too subjective.

The Leo child is stubborn and fixed. He is going to emulate his father. The Leo child is trusting, enthusiastic, and open—it's hard to deflate him. But if he feels put down, he gets very hurt. There is a dichotomy here—he's stubborn, but if he needs correction, his ego and self-esteem suffer. As masterful as he can be, he still needs lots of affection.

Partnerships

Leo needs a mate. Regardless of whom he picks as a partner, the Leo male has excellent staying power, and this will extend to the family—he's the big daddy. His partnerships and commitments are strong.

The Leo female, on the other hand, is just the opposite. If a partner doesn't meet her standards, she will start to bully, expect change, and project her need to control right onto her partner.

If you're involved with a Leo, recognize that this is a demanding individual. You need to approach Leo with tenderness if you don't want him to roar. In handling a Leo, it helps to explain, in a gentle way, what your needs are—never demand.

DECANS

FIRST DECAN: **Leo/Leo**—(0 to 10 degrees or approximately July 23–August 2)

This vital Sun quality is ambitious, straightforward, and dignified. Leo is also a good friend who is loyal beyond the call of duty. This decan also enjoys the good life—good times, good fellows, and good old fun.

If afflicted, this becomes a roaring lion—one who will not forgive and who will seek to avenge. Leo/Leo can interpret reprimands as indignations and is extremely self-conscious. This creates the inability to move to a more positive attitude. Lessons are harder for this Leo because of his self-righteousness. Leo is also embarrassed by his limitations. He hides this well, but all it does is compound the problem for him.

SECOND DECAN: **Leo/Sagittarius**—(10 to 20 degrees or approximately August 3–12)

This Leo, with the flavor of Sagittarius and Jupiter, is philosophical and cautious. He knows that there is more to life than material surroundings and immediate gratification. He is sociable, friendly, open, and aboveboard.

Should there be an affliction, the Jupiter influence will overexpand, and Leo will become bombastic and make promises he can't keep.

THIRD DECAN: **Leo/Aries**—(20 to 30 degrees or approximately August 13–22)

Mars energizes everything it touches. Therefore, when the Sun combines with the energy of Aries/Mars, this becomes a powerful Leo. This Leo can override his stubbornness. He can become courageous, independent, energized, and majestic in the truest sense of the word.

If afflicted, it can create someone who is afraid, who has a seed of doubt, and must deal with rejection or the fear of rejection.

VIRGO (AUGUST 23–SEPTEMBER 22)

Symbol—The Virgin
Ruling Planet—Mercury
Element—Earth
Cross—Mutable
Group—Intellectual
Gender—Feminine

House Ruled—Sixth

Famous Virgos—Beyoncé, Mother Teresa, Queen Elizabeth I, Kobe Bryant, D. H. Lawrence, Prince Harry, Michael Jackson, Idris Elba, H. G. Wells, Stephen King

Basic Personality

Virgo is methodical, talented, and hardworking. She is discriminating, tasteful, and reserved. Because she is ruled by Mercury, Virgo can examine things both abstractly and concretely. Highly intelligent and creative, she uses her analytical ability to see both sides of the coin. She is orderly and structured. And because she is mutable, Virgo quickly adapts to any environment.

On the negative side, Virgo can be carping, rigid, and critical. That wonderful Mercurial quality will turn sarcastic, making her the master of the put-down, condemning others to justify her imperfections.

Because she is an earth sign, Virgo is a methodical planner who refuses input from other people. She can become snobbish and narrow-minded, discarding whomever she does not consider intellectual enough for her standards. This occurs because Virgo worries about intellectual contamination. She gravitates only to those whom she considers her "equals." With maturity, Virgo will hopefully realize that there is a difference between analysis and criticism. But until then, she takes everything as criticism.

Virgo has an underlying fear of success. She is aware that success can also bring notoriety and is more comfortable behind the scenes and working alone. Virgo is not motivated by fame and the limelight but by her basic need to achieve and accomplish something of importance and value—something she can take pride in.

Talents and Abilities

Virgo is talented, intelligent, and successful at whatever career or long-term goals she desires. She takes on enormous responsibility and is as hardworking as the day is long.

Virgo rules the sixth house, the house of health, which makes her successful in the medical field, whether as a doctor, nurse, or administrator.

Virgo is a superb communicator and excels in education, teaching, and writing.

Health and Physical Traits

Virgo rules the intestinal tract. Her food cannot be adulterated or else her body quickly responds with stomach or intestinal ailments. Virgo is also prone to food-related allergies.

Although Virgo possesses a self-healing ability, ironically, she also has a tendency toward hypochondria. She is obsessed with germs and won't drink out of someone else's glass or use a public toilet without first covering the seat. If afflicted, this concern with cleanliness might make her obsessive-compulsive about dirt and give her a severe fear of contamination. This makes Virgo feel vulnerable to all illnesses—both physical and mental.

Family Relationships

Virgo comes from a household where condemnation, especially by the father, is predominant. Her father will demand and condemn, and so Virgo starts condemning others to justify her own imperfections. She is convinced that nothing and no one is perfect, including herself.

The mother is influential to the basic personality of Virgo, so much so that attitudes about partners and the world are derived from the mother as well. Unfortunately, a Virgo's mother often has a critical or condescending attitude about Dad. Virgo needs to distance herself from this parental difficulty. If not, she'll develop trouble in love affairs and marriage because she will wind up feeling superior to and competitive with her mate. Virgo needs to work out her issues with her father—her outlooks on life and love depend on it.

The Virgo mother is meticulous—a little bit demanding, especially as her children get older. She has an enormous caring that equates to the setting of good standards. Though she appears to be loving and caring, she tends to demonstrate it in an intellectual rather than physical or emotional manner.

The Virgo father is a quietly roaming nonentity in a household. He really doesn't bother with children until they are much older and he can converse with them on an equal footing. At that point, he becomes more involved and responsive. More often than not, he's like a shadow who will only be heard from when he is displeased.

Both parents must be careful not to invalidate the accomplishments of their children. If a child brings home a test score of 95, the Virgo parent tends to ask why it wasn't 100—to compare it to something greater or someone else's achievements.

Partnerships

This is the only Sun Sign that can successfully marry its own sign. Two Virgos can have a long and happy marriage. They know how to self-analyze and adjust.

Although Virgo has many inhibitions, she still possesses a passionate quality. Once those inhibitions are shed, her passion knows no boundaries.

Because Virgo is dominated by Mother and has issues to work out with Father, relationship problems often exist. The Virgo male, in particular, always seeks perfection in his mate. This is a difficult quandary for Virgo. He needs simply to accept and feel love and not analyze it or look for certainty. Love is something that cannot be analyzed—it must be felt to blossom and succeed.

DECANS

FIRST DECAN: **Virgo/Virgo**—(0 to 10 degrees or approximately August 23–September 1)

With a double Mercury rulership, this decan of Virgo is quiet and shy with a tremendous need for solitude. She needs to learn to overcome loneliness and self-imposed isolation by accepting others rather than fearing them or shutting them out.

SECOND DECAN: **Virgo/Capricorn**—(10 to 20 degrees or approximately September 2–11)

Capricorn and Saturn tend to make for serious thinking. Virgo in this decan can be an excellent teacher or healer.

This Virgo takes nothing for granted. She is basically inhibited and serious and never assumes or presumes—she tests and earns it. Virgo knows she must work for everything but also knows that she will reap the benefits at the end of the line. She is not looking for fame, notoriety, or adulation but for security and a clean reputation.

If afflicted, there is an increase in moodiness, isolation, rigidity, and one-sidedness in this native.

THIRD DECAN: **Virgo/Taurus**—(20 to 30 degrees or approximately September 12–22)

Because Virgo is flavored by Taurus and Venus, she tends to be more fun-loving, friendly, and less compulsive in this decan. She might not always enjoy the routine of everyday work but will find a creative outlet. This decan of Virgo also tends to have a flair for acting.

LIBRA (SEPTEMBER 23-OCTOBER 23)

Symbol—The Scales
Ruling Planet—Venus
Element—Air
Cross—Cardinal

Group—Intellectual
Gender—Masculine
House Ruled—Seventh
Famous Librans—John Lennon, Oscar Wilde, Will Smith,
F. Scott Fitzgerald, Mahatma Gandhi, Sting, Kamala Harris,
Serena Williams, Hugh Jackman, Dwight D. Eisenhower

Basic Personality

Libra is a happy, generous, and realistic individual. Although a masculine sign, the rulership of Venus gives Libra an edge of refinement and femininity.

Libra is charming, amiable, gracious, and affectionate. As the sign of the scales, he is looking to keep a balance. He has a rare and important gift—he is a natural mediator who can objectively see both sides of the coin, making him the world's best judge. This ability to think impartially also makes Libra a great strategist. Libra sits back, examines every possibility and probability, devises a plan, and then acts. He has the foresight to see what the other person is going to do or what the next move is.

Libra is a materialist. There is little spirituality in Libra; in fact, he's quite superficial in that area. If his ego is weak, he can also be self-indulgent, like the caricature of the bonbon-eating lady on a satin sofa. Venus's rulership influences this native to amass material purely for the sake of reassurance and security. He can overindulge in food and sex as well.

Libra's ego is extremely vulnerable. When his equilibrium

is balanced, he's fine; when it's not, he is easily hurt, worrisome, and anxious. Libra rules the seventh house, which is the house of partnerships, so he often looks for approval from his partners, and if he doesn't get it, he becomes depressed. He doesn't like to be alone and needs a partner to feel whole. If Libra is afflicted, he will latch on to one partner after another; it doesn't matter who it is, as long as someone is there. Libra needs to develop self-reliance to strengthen his ego.

Libra wants peace at any price. He will compromise and suppress his feelings or hostilities for the sake of creating harmony. Libra gives up or gives in because he fears confrontation. This is not healthy because swallowing anger and repressing emotions can negatively affect Libra's health and well-being.

This tendency toward suppression also makes Libra forgetful. He may sometimes give the impression of being scatterbrained, but Libra is actually an intelligent human being who is simply avoiding. When Libra drops out, he retreats into counterproductive fantasy and illusion.

When Libra is positive, he has wonderful mental balance and mental health. Air signs are mental people—concepts and ideas people. When well balanced, Libra is capable and accomplishes a great deal. When his innate sense of detachment and impartiality is favorably maximized, Libra can objectively view his ideas and feelings and intelligently decide whether they are worth pursuing.

Talents and Abilities

Libra possesses courage. There are many famous Libra generals and strategists—Dwight D. Eisenhower, for example. Libra has the fortitude and strategic aptitude to achieve success on the front lines. The ability to detach and impersonalize, influenced by the refinement of Venus, also makes Libra an excellent diplomat.

Libra's impartiality and balance make him a superb judge or mediator in the field of law. Most judges have a prominent Libra house, position, or several Libra planets in their charts.

Libra also excels in any field that requires a sense of symmetry or a keen eye for color—like interior decorating or photography. Libra can pass a picture hanging on a wall, notice that it's out of kilter by an eighth of an inch, and automatically straighten it out.

Health and Physical Traits

Libra rules the kidneys and the blood. He has a sweet tooth and must be mindful of his pancreas and diet. As an air sign, Libra tends to be dry and should regularly consume liquids. Drinking a lot of clear water is beneficial to his health.

Libra can develop kidney stones or other kidney difficulties. The liver is also at risk if he is not careful about his health.

Because of Libra's need for mental balance, if negatively afflicted, he can suffer from mental illness, sometimes as severe as schizophrenia or catatonia. When Libra is mentally ill, he can withdraw completely from reality.

Family Relationships

Libra is often born into strange circumstances and is frequently the product of unwed parents. If he is born to a married couple, most likely, the father is rarely there; he's either a workaholic or on the road.

The Libra mother views her children as reflections of herself. She enjoys primping and fussing over them and is generous, loving, and proud of her children.

The Libra father, on the other hand, is inferior. He competes for attention with his children—he will even upstage his children to get noticed. He also lacks assertiveness. When it comes to discipline, he prefers for someone else to take the reins.

The Libra child is not consciously aware of tension in the household—he senses it in the gut. There is usually dissension between his parents, and that makes him quiet and withdrawn. He wants his parents to treat each other with respect and kindness. If there are overt marital tensions in the household, the Libra child will transcend the family and disassociate.

The Libra child is usually afraid to be alone—doesn't like to sleep alone, won't go to the bathroom by himself. He feels insecure and incomplete. This is a difficult placement for an only child.

In general, Libra is a quiet and darling child who is cooperative and eager to please. He is bright, perceptive, and wants to fit in. He avoids making waves or getting in the middle of controversy. The Libra child will not display anger or disappointment and might even smile when crying. However, as he matures, he will start to recognize and feel anger and hurt. Sooner or later, Libra must learn to stand up and be counted.

Partnerships

Libra is an affectionate sign; he is loving and demonstrative but tends to fall in love with love. The Libra female is refined and loving, but if she finds that her "knight in shining armor" is rusted, she can fall out of love in an instant. She gets bored with her partner, and unless he can really hold her to the relationship, she is going to stray and have many partners or affairs.

The Libra male has many of the same qualities as the female. He, too, gets easily bored. He can lose himself in his career or other stimulating pursuits. He is easygoing, sociable, and prone to extramarital affairs. The Libra man prefers women who are self-sufficient, professional, and interested in work and achievements outside the home. He does not want to be bogged down with mundane details of life and is stimulated by an exciting and productive partner.

Libra rules the seventh house, which is the house of marriage and partnership, but that does not guarantee consistency. Laziness is a big problem for Libra. He can get bored with a partner and wind up in and out of marriages. Libra wants excitement and is always looking for "more."

DECANS

FIRST DECAN: **Libra/Libra**—(0 to 10 degrees or approximately September 23–October 2)

The double Venus quality makes for a pleasant disposition. Venus produces an enormous power of attraction; he's refined and cultured and going to enchant people. Yet it's a quality that works strictly for the "self."

Libra is artistic in this decan and can work well with others. He can make an excellent social worker.

SECOND DECAN: **Libra/Aquarius**—(10 to 20 degrees or approximately October 3–13)

This is an unconventional Libra who is strong-minded and willing to stick his neck out. Aquarius is ruled by Uranus, which is daring and a power wielder. The male in this decan has natural agility and the leadership qualities to run a successful organization. The female sometimes becomes a bit too masculine in this situation and doesn't always feel comfortable or happy. She might develop an aggressive edge that conflicts with both her innate character and the refined influence of Venus.

THIRD DECAN: **Libra/Gemini**—(20 to 30 degrees or approximately October 14–23)

The influence of Gemini/Mercury gives this Libra an

inquisitiveness and curiosity that lends itself to investigative careers or journalism. This Libra is out there getting the scoop and is always on the go. He has an abundance of energy and knows how to pace himself and achieve results without exhausting himself. When these talents are combined with physical attractiveness (which is prevalent in this decan), Libra can also find success as a television reporter or anchorperson.

SCORPIO (OCTOBER 24– NOVEMBER 21)

Symbol—The Scorpion
Ruling Planet—Pluto/Mars
Element—Water
Cross—Fixed
Group—Intellectual
Gender—Feminine
House Ruled—Fifth
Famous Scorpions—Prince Charles, Gordon Ramsay, Marie Curie, Julia Roberts, Pablo Picasso, Billy Graham, Charles Manson, Theodore Roosevelt, Bill Gates, Hillary Clinton

Basic Personality
Scorpio rules one of the houses of the soul. She rules the genitals, too, and because of that, there have been more weird stories about Scorpio than you can shake a stick at.

Scorpio is a dual-planet sign. Its ancient rulership was Mars, but in 1930, the planet Pluto was discovered, and its erratic qualities were applied to Scorpio. As a result, there is a Scorpio that answers to a Mars vibration and a Scorpio that answers to a Pluto vibration. That accounts for her passions and extremes.

When it comes to Scorpio, it's black or white. When it comes to Scorpio, it's love or hate. She doesn't want you to like her; she wants you to love her. And if you can't love her, she would rather you hate her. There is no in-between.

Scorpio is purposeful. She is directed and dominant. She's a feminine water sign with strong, covert energy. Scorpio emanates a potent aura that is the height of magnetism. She is emotional but also possesses an intellectual and persuasive power that is best illustrated, at its most negative level, by Charles Manson—that is how powerful this Scorpio can be. It is a power that can create fear. On the other hand, in a more positive light, there is Billy Graham, a man who has moved thousands of people with his faith.

Scorpio is hugely ambitious, fearless, and self-sufficient. At the negative level, though, she's a bully. Love, hate, anger, fear—these emotions run through her in full force, making her hostile, cynical, and self-righteous. Have you ever seen a Scorpio brooding? She's menacing. And vengeful. *Vendetta* is a word created for Scorpio. She holds hostilities and grudges, and even if it takes twenty years, she will seek her revenge.

Scorpio has death anxiety. She rules the eighth house,

and this is where Pluto comes in—the planet of death/re-birth. Scorpio frequently contends with death. Whether it be the untimely death of a parent, a sibling, a mate, or a friend, invariably, death will impact and influence her life.

Under the best circumstances, Scorpio can be protective of others, but if afflicted, possessiveness takes over. She becomes jealous and subsequently competitive—she wants to beat everybody and be the best. She's arrogant, brilliant, and dangerous. She becomes prideful and starts to identify herself through material possessions and relationships with others. It creates an insecurity that can lead to stinginess and condemnation. The "I am the master, you are the slave," concept lies in the heart of Scorpio. She manifests this in partnerships, predominantly romantic relationships or marriage. Scorpio is possessive and controlling of others because she is afraid of rejection. An afflicted Scorpio hides her insecurities well.

The unconscious force that drives Scorpio is her free-flowing energy. It heightens her sexual drive. This is a person without inhibitions. Her ego has one motive and that is to be responsible for the self. Her sexuality is pure energy, and when afflicted, she becomes erotically obsessed. Scorpio lacks a censoring device, so she doesn't care how her energy and sexuality impact others—she has no guilt and is highly self-indulgent.

At a positive level, she can sublimate this powerful, sexual energy to produce healing. Scorpio has enormous healing abilities. She not only regenerates herself but helps others as well. This healing can be accomplished through religion, therapeutic guidance, or medicine.

Talents and Abilities

Scorpio is the world's best imitator—if she sees you doing it once, she will do you one better. She has an incredible ability to learn and has great mental retention—she can instantly recall information and events.

Scorpio's powerful healing abilities make her an excellent doctor, surgeon, or diagnostician. She also makes a shrewd detective—Scorpio will look at you and see right through to the truth.

Scorpio is not as involved with ideas as with the power of ideas. She has executive qualities and enormous magnetism, which might even make her a good politician.

Health and Physical Traits

Scorpio usually has no inhibitions, but should there be, she will manifest them through physical difficulty. If there is a suppression of energy and a deviation in her normal bodily flows, she can develop heart problems.

Scorpio is a sign of excess. She has difficulty with self-control and will often overindulge in food or sex. Since Scorpio rules the genitals, males might experience prostate problems. Good health is dependent on exercise, something Scorpio dislikes.

Family Relationships

Scorpio comes into the world with rejection. Her father probably didn't want her, and her mother might not have wanted the pregnancy (particularly true of a Scorpio Moon placement). If this is the case, Scorpio innately knows it and is driven to compensate for that rejection. When she is born, she comes out swinging. This is something that Scorpio must learn to curb and overcome.

The Scorpio mother is poor. She is possessive and demanding of her children and finds it difficult to let them grow up. She is not particularly generous either. With a Scorpio mother, you've got to get your own and earn it yourself.

Fathers do a little bit better. Strangely enough, the Scorpio father is a more patient and determined dad than other Sun Signs. He has a good understanding of children, particularly his own. If afflicted, however, he will look at his children as a reflection of himself and have enormous but often unrealistic expectations of them.

The Scorpio child has many needs and will be boisterous about them. She is demanding and competitive, especially with siblings. If she can't get her needs met by her own family, the Scorpio child will find someone else's family to bond with.

This child is a natural brooder who can't sit still. She's a tough child who will not be placated. It is helpful for her to move and keep busy. An intelligent and perceptive child, Scorpio needs mental and physical stimulation. The Scorpio boy often takes his mother for granted, expecting her to take care of all his needs. As an adult, he winds up expecting his wife to do the same.

Partnerships

Scorpio is prideful and often identifies herself through others. This is dangerous because, in many cases, Scorpio chooses a spouse not out of love but because she has the right qualities to reflect or represent her mate.

Even the best Scorpio is not a romantic. Partners are chosen purely for ego positions. For Scorpio, there is no equality in a relationship—she must be in charge and be the king or queen. This is how she asserts and identifies herself.

When Scorpio takes on a partner and family, she absorbs them and they become part of her. She is highly possessive; what is hers is truly hers, and she cannot let go. Even when divorced, Scorpio is still not mentally divorced—she won't give up anything, which makes it hard for her to establish new relationships.

The Scorpio female also has a strong ego. She has the notion that if she sexually satisfies a man, he will never go elsewhere. The Scorpio female doesn't fall in love. Although down-to-earth, she is demanding and thinks sex is a power that is endless. Once married, she is as possessive as the male.

The inability to strike an ego balance with a partner is the reason why Scorpio's relationships go askew. The best advice to Scorpio for a stable relationship is to learn to respect and consider your partner.

DECANS

FIRST DECAN: **Scorpio/Scorpio**—(0 to 10 degrees or approximately October 24–November 2)

Scorpio/Scorpio is an outwardly calm but secretive individual.

Scorpio in this decan has a lack of polish. She is competitive and uses her will instead of strategy to get ahead. She can get pushy and has little concern for the consequences of her actions.

SECOND DECAN: **Scorpio/Pisces**—(10 to 20 degrees or approximately November 3–12)

With the influence of Pisces/Neptune, this Scorpio needs to be elevated; she needs philosophical concepts and ethics. She must learn to take all her magnificent qualities and serve the world. By serving, through professional achievement or humanistic endeavors, Scorpio will avoid stinging others and, inevitably, herself.

THIRD DECAN: **Scorpio/Cancer**—(20 to 30 degrees or approximately November 13–21)

Scorpio has now taken on the Moon quality of Cancer, and this is Scorpio at her softest. She makes an excellent psychologist or psychiatrist because the Moon/Pluto combination creates a remarkable ability to empathize and sympathize, and bestow a psychic kindness on others.

SAGITTARIUS (NOVEMBER 22–DECEMBER 21)

Symbol—The Archer
Ruling Planet—Jupiter
Element—Fire
Cross—Mutable
Group—Theoretical
Gender—Masculine
House Ruled—Ninth
Famous Sagittarians—Taylor Swift, Winston Churchill, Mark Twain, Walt Disney, Jane Austen, Ludwig van Beethoven, Brad Pitt, Billie Eilish, Steven Spielberg, Frank Sinatra

Basic Personality

Sagittarius has been given, by his ruling planet of Jupiter, an extraordinary gift of intuition. It's a gut feeling, a "knowing without knowing," because it is not intellectually or educationally based. It is an intuition that is equated with luck.

Sagittarius is honest. He's versatile and optimistic, independent, and friendly. In fact, Sagittarius considers even the most casual acquaintance his friend.

Considered the "sign of the millionaire," most people

born under the sign of Sagittarius have a high IQ and are achievement-driven.

Sagittarius also has a healthy, unconscious mechanism that keeps his psyche well adjusted. At a positive level, this person is devoid of fear and neuroses. Sagittarius thrives on freedom and independence. A freewheeling individual, he has no inhibitions. He does not suppress or repress emotions like other Sun Signs.

If he is afflicted, however, he loses his competitive edge and drive. He will begin to suffer from doubt and then find it hard to trust his instincts. He can start feeling claustrophobic, which can lead to wanderlust. In that state of mind, he thinks only of himself and begins eliminating his responsibilities. Sagittarius must learn that to achieve autonomy, he must meet his obligations first.

The ninth house, ruled by Sagittarius, is the house of theories, concepts, and philosophy. Quite often, Sagittarius thinks his perception is the only one. He must deal with the fact that his truth is not the ultimate truth.

Sagittarius is a theoretical sign with the ability for abstract thinking. He can understand and decipher that which is not tangible. A creative individual, he can go beyond the limitations of touching, feeling, and seeing. He conceives things before they have been manifested. The inherent difficulty for Sagittarius is that because he's the one who has keen perception, he must take his ideas and instincts and bring them forth in a way that others can perceive and understand.

When Sagittarius is afflicted, he becomes rebellious and irresponsible. He gets careless about what he says, becoming extremely inaccurate and superficial, with little regard to his words or actions. He doesn't know how to hold his tongue, becomes impulsive and outspoken without stopping to deliberate. Even in a positive mode, he feels compelled to express himself candidly. You don't have to ask Sagittarius to tell you the truth—he will, whether you want to hear it or not. Sagittarius is unaware of the effects this has on others. Never argue or get into a heated discussion with a Sagittarius—he gets personal and attacks you at your weakest point. He will undermine you so that he can win the argument, whether he is right or wrong.

If Sagittarius is chided for his outspokenness or if you can't see his sense of humor or handle him with a sense of humor, he lapses into resignation, which is comparable to defeat. His drive diminishes and he becomes emotionally and mentally sloppy, careless, indifferent—all the qualities of someone whose fire and spirit have been dampened.

The restrictions, limitations, and discipline of Sagittarius should be handled carefully and philosophically. He sees everything as a challenge. Although he is theoretical, he doesn't always follow or conform to his own philosophies.

Talents and Abilities

Since the ninth house is where religion and philosophy enter, Sagittarius can make a fine man of the cloth—minister, priest, nun, or rabbi. His innate sense of abstract vision allows him to excel as an engineer, architect, or general contractor.

His natural sense of the absurd makes him a good comedian, and his personable manner makes him comfortable in sales. He thrives in any career that allows him freedom of movement.

A natural gambler, Sagittarius is always game to tackle something new. He is able and capable and carries a professional attitude toward his work.

Health and Physical Traits

Sagittarius rules the hips, sciatic nerve, and liver. Since he is a mutable sign, he tends to have allergies, usually related to grains like wheat or barley. Diet is important. Sagittarius doesn't take much interest in food; he eats to live but needs to be careful about what he eats or drinks. With a sensitive liver, it is recommended that Sagittarius abstain from alcohol, particularly grain-based liquors.

Sagittarius is mentally and physically self-regulating. He possesses the ability to heal his body through his mind. If afflicted, he loses that ability and can no longer control his body or his psyche.

Naturally athletic and competitive, exercise is of great benefit to Sagittarius but should not be overdone. He needs to be careful about running because it could be damaging or stressful to the hips. Swimming is an excellent alternative.

Family Relationships

The Sagittarius mother is reasonably good, but she doesn't like to have her lifestyle cramped. If she is not too obsessed with the need for personal independence, she can guide her children well and provide them with insight. She can make an excellent mother who will encourage and empower her children to great heights. She provides for her children but takes care of her needs, too. If she feels claustrophobic or that her freedom is being hampered, she can begin to neglect everything and everyone around her, including herself.

The Sagittarian father is an out-and-out poor parent. Homelife is not a priority to him because it restricts his freedom and independence.

The Sagittarius female tends to compete with her sister(s) for her father's (or even her brother's) attention. She is looking for approval from Dad, who, unfortunately, will probably never give it unless she has a good mother to help encourage Dad's support.

The Sagittarius child is bright, tall, lean, and very quick. This is an active and social kid, gregarious, happy by nature, talkative, and animated. The Sagittarius child is intelligent and has a high IQ, regardless of his parents' intellect or success. Sagittarius is a father-dominated sign, and the Sagittarius child can be in a bad state if he has a father who does not accept him or who will compete with him. This is particularly difficult for a little boy—he may feel like he doesn't measure up, and his father will challenge him rather than empower him.

When he succeeds, the Sagittarius child can become depressed—he has outdone his father and might incur his wrath. He might even develop a fear of success due to his concern about how it will impact his relationship with his father.

Partnerships

When the Sagittarian male gets married, he becomes a married bachelor. He thinks his wife is the one who is married, not him. He makes decisions predicated on his needs and expects his wife to go along. He is not romantic and is quite spontaneous about sex—when he wants it, he wants it now, and his interest must be maintained. The Sagittarius male doesn't trust women. His involvement with Dad often took precedence over his relationship with and the value of his mother, which winds up impairing his relationships with women. Sagittarius doesn't understand women and is basically chauvinistic. He has a partner in theory, and his relationships will remain stable as long as his partner meets all his "shoulds"; if she doesn't, he'll roam. He's a good provider, but that's it. He expects his mate to be available, consistent, and tolerant of his needs and wants, but he's not particularly trustworthy. He doesn't have what it takes to be a good partner.

The Sagittarius female, who grows up seeking her father's approval, will transfer that dynamic to other men. She is competitive with other women for the attentions of men and will subsequently select a partner she can also compete with. She is not the dependent type.

DECANS

FIRST DECAN: **Sagittarius/Sagittarius**—(0 to 10 degrees or approximately November 22–December 1)

This Sagittarius is talkative, restless, and interesting, and makes a superb salesman. He is sociable, entertaining, and pleasant to be around. If afflicted, he becomes careless and sloppy—a liar, a gossip, and just plain manipulative.

SECOND DECAN: **Sagittarius/Aries**—(10 to 20 degrees or approximately December 2–11)

This decan is adventurous and a risk-taker. He's the explorer who boarded the ship and sailed to the New World. Whatever he undertakes is important and necessary—he has a faith in himself that makes him able to be courageous, take chances, and, ultimately, achieve.

If afflicted, the adventurous nature of this Sagittarius will simply lead to foolhardiness.

THIRD DECAN: **Sagittarius/Leo**—(20 to 30 degrees or approximately December 12–21)

This is a powerful placement that almost guarantees success. Sagittarius is, in general, a successful sign, and if he isn't, it is through either his own undoing or an affliction that has not been overcome. The power of Leo combined with the intuitive power of Jupiter provides Sagittarius with an innate homing device that lets him know where to go, what to do, when to do it, and how to do it, regardless of others' support or belief in him. This is a strong position for fame and fortune.

CAPRICORN (DECEMBER 22–JANUARY 19)

Symbol—The Goat
Ruling Planet—Saturn
Element—Earth
Cross—Cardinal
Group—Theoretical
Gender—Feminine
House Ruled—Tenth
Famous Capricorns—Elvis Presley, Richard Nixon, Martin Luther King Jr., Benjamin Franklin, Joan of Arc, Isaac Newton, Dolly Parton, Muhammad Ali, Michelle Obama, Greta Thunberg

Basic Personality

Capricorn is determined, single-minded, and possesses directed energy. She doesn't fantasize, she visualizes. Capricorn will envision a goal, impress it in her mind, hold it dear to her heart, then carry through until that goal or desire is realized.

Because of Saturn's rulership, Capricorn is serious and seldom considered magnetic. Impressive, yes, but not magnetic. She is somewhat self-centered with an overdeveloped ego that gives her a high sense of responsibility. She can be extremely austere, relentless without observing, ruthless, and opportunistic. Capricorn can exercise a sense of denial that allows her to win under any circumstance.

Capricorn has an inferiority complex that she compensates for by striving to maintain a strong public image. When she is in conflict, she can become egocentric, lapsing into a selfishness of distorted proportions, whereby becoming convinced of her omnipotence.

Since Capricorn is in the polarity of starvation, her innate fear of starvation makes her hoard. She is not generous by nature and needs to learn how to share.

Several unconscious motives direct Capricorn. The first is a retentiveness that makes her downright stingy. The second is anxiety about loss or failure. Even when Capricorn is aggressive, she is always defensive. If afflicted, she becomes rigid. This inability to bend is accentuated by the repression of all impulses, making her unable to move forward. This is a troubling conflict for Capricorn given her innate and phenomenal strength and tenacity.

Capricorn is serious and very aware of her reputation. She is a planner and an enabler and will make many sacrifices to attain her goals. Single-minded, she systematically moves forward. The keyword for Capricorn is *respect*. She believes that payback comes through hard work and is a stickler for playing by the rules.

Talents and Abilities

Capricorn is an excellent organizer. Her strong leadership skills and goal-oriented attitude can make her an effective chief executive of a major company.

Capricorn has a wonderful aptitude for math, which allows her to shine in banking, finance, real estate, building, or general contracting. Her abilities are best placed under her command since she knows where and how money is to be made.

Health and Physical Traits

Capricorn rules the skeletal structure, bones, and spinal column. Capricorn tends to be tall, but her knees and spine are vulnerable, and she generally has problems with posture.

Capricorn often has a loss of body calcium and needs to supplement calcium in her diet. This is necessary to maintain the integrity of her bones and teeth, which can suffer if her diet is not rich in calcium.

Family Relationships

This is probably one of the most mother-dominated signs of all. If you look at a Capricorn, you usually see her mother, both physically and in character.

The Capricorn mother must watch that she doesn't become all work and no play. She can be harsh with her children but also protective. The Capricorn father is basically domineering and always worried about what "people will say."

The Capricorn child is like an old person—serious and responsible. Ironically, as she matures, she retains her youth. Capricorn truly looks and gets better as she gets older.

The Capricorn child is resourceful. She'll deliver newspapers or set up a lemonade stand to earn money to buy her own bicycle. Since she is mother-dominated, Capricorn will even go out and buy Mom what she needs. A Capricorn boy often wants to get rid of Dad—he doesn't understand why Mom needs him and wants to take Dad's place. He is protective of his mother and deems his father useless. He frequently winds up becoming his own father.

Partnerships

Capricorn has deep passions for human relationships. If she softens her retentiveness and inhibitions, she has boundless energy.

The Capricorn male is protective. He is not particularly romantic and not a playboy. He needs a wife and family. He is prone to marrying for social status, so his wife must come from a polished, well-educated, respectable family—he doesn't want scandals emerging from the past.

The Capricorn female is not fixated on the physical attractiveness of her mate—she is more interested in someone with a successful career, a future, money, and respectability rather than lust or romance. She wants a man who can afford her and who is a good provider.

Capricorn can be loving, although not demonstrative. She can be in love and inwardly passionate but is usually not good at showing it. It takes a rare partner to bring those qualities to the surface.

DECANS

FIRST DECAN: **Capricorn/Capricorn**—(0 to 10 degrees or approximately December 22–31)

The keyword is *ambition*. Capricorn in this decan is a meticulous planner who always has an objective—she can't live without one. True to her symbol, she's that mountain goat climbing straight up the hill, and if she slips a bit, she will climb right back up again. If afflicted, she will think in terms of her own needs and desires, which will drive her to the point of climbing that mountain so fast she'll darn well fall right off it. Saturn has a way of making sure that everything gained is earned. If Capricorn manipulates, bypasses the ground rules, or is unethical, she'll fall from the highest place. That is guaranteed.

SECOND DECAN: **Capricorn/Taurus**—(10 to 20 degrees or approximately January 1–10)

The combination of Saturn/Venus can be softening to austere Capricorn. It allows her some self-love, which she's not prone to naturally. Venus is going to give her a quality that attracts. Females in this decan are particularly pretty. They have a balance and structure to their appearance that is not usually present with Saturn.

If afflicted, Capricorn is going to be egocentric, self-centered, and self-serving. She will be her own worst enemy, which could lead to her undoing.

THIRD DECAN: **Capricorn/Virgo**—(20 to 30 degrees or approximately January 11–19)

This combination makes Capricorn discriminating and intellectual, with a quickness of mind that borders on brilliance. In this decan, Capricorn makes an excellent accountant, teacher, or journalist—the type you send out to get the news, which she does efficiently.

If afflicted, this Capricorn will be critical and demanding. While she will be a good, hard worker, she will also expect everybody else to meet her standards. This is an individual who works more effectively alone.

AQUARIUS (JANUARY 20– FEBRUARY 18)

Symbol—The Water Bearer

Ruling Planet—Uranus/Saturn

Element—Air

Cross—Fixed

Group—Theoretical

Gender—Masculine

House Ruled—Eleventh

Famous Aquarians—Oprah Winfrey, Charles Darwin, Galileo, Franklin D. Roosevelt, Abraham Lincoln, Thomas Edison, Charles Dickens, Norman Rockwell, Ellen DeGeneres, Michael Jordan

Basic Personality

Aquarius is often called *the humanistic sign*. Personable, he gets along with almost anyone. He is imaginative, generous, and often inspiring.

Aquarius is practical and always looking to improve the self. Before Uranus ruled Aquarius, it was Saturn ruled, and Saturn makes sure that one becomes self-aware.

Aquarius has insights ahead of his time. He can tap into the experience and knowledge of generations, which is stored in his collective unconscious. For Aquarius, knowledge is not for his self-preservation but for the preservation of all man. His foresight enables him to go into the future. Since he must reconcile the past to get into the future, it creates a conflict—past versus future—back and forth inside his head. As a result, he needs to strike a mental balance and acquire boundaries to avoid confusion or the type of abstract thinking that makes him unable to maintain his feet on the ground.

As a theoretical sign, Aquarius can ascend to a sophisticated mental level and become woolly headed, obstinate, and antisocial. He can unintentionally isolate himself through preoccupation with his thoughts or endeavors. Occasionally, Aquarius becomes morbidly focused on unconventionality. He will create conflict and go against society, the environment, current morality, and so on, simply to challenge or shatter the status quo.

Aquarius is impressionable and easily swayed by others. The selection of his environment and peers is critical and influential to his healthy and productive development.

In a strong and positive position, Aquarius can be the most rational of individuals. Since he has the gift of foresight and prophecy, his insight into other human beings can, ultimately, make him tactful and considerate.

Talents and Abilities

Aquarius shines in service industries. His excellent socialization skills allow him to succeed in any field that brings him in contact with other people, whether it be social work, humanitarian pursuits, public relations, or politics. Many American presidents have been born under the sign of Aquarius.

Aquarius excels at anything that involves mental stimulation or thinking. He can succeed in any electronics-related field. He makes an excellent engineer, scientist, inventor, electrician, or x-ray technician.

Health and Physical Traits

Aquarius rules the ankles, the cardiovascular system, and circulation. By nature, he is not a physical being—you've got to get him up off his butt and moving because he tends to be contemplative and physically inert. It is beneficial for Aquarius to keep his diet light and get regular exercise.

Since he tends to overwork his mind, if he does not strike a balance between body and mind, Aquarius must watch out for mental breakdowns. The heady, mental qualities of Aquarius, when afflicted, can produce a loss of boundaries and a risk of psychological withdrawal.

Family Relationships

The Aquarian mother is generally unimpressive. She is occasionally good, but that depends on her willingness to accept routines that Aquarius doesn't like. She tends to be a mediocre homemaker—housekeeping is not her forte.

Unless other planets influence the chart, she is basically sloppy. The reason she isn't meticulous or domestically adept is that her mind is usually elsewhere.

The Aquarius father is poor, too. Parenting from an Aquarius father is, at best, permissive. Like the mother, the father also doesn't care for routine and repetition. He will indulge his child in any way as long as he is not bothered. Although Aquarian parents genuinely love their children, they are not particularly meticulous about child-rearing in general.

The Aquarius child is independent but loves socializing with others. This is a little contradictory—he wants to be alone but doesn't want to be alone. You should be mindful of the Aquarian child because he will begin to identify with his friends and do exactly what they are doing. He needs to establish his own identity, as opposed to going along with the crowd.

The Aquarius child also needs to be mentally engaged. He doesn't always pay attention to what is going on or being said and will often only listen to part of a request. He lacks patience and easily becomes bored and oblivious. He needs to work at remembering things and beefing up his recall. Even a traumatic experience will be forgotten by an Aquarius child.

Maturity and sophistication can elevate this child, but he must be kept in school. Although he hates routines, he must be encouraged to stick it out, particularly where education is concerned. It will all pay off to his benefit in the end.

Partnerships

Aquarius is often tall, lean, attractive, and not short of partners. He is romantic and enjoys anything that strokes his emotions. Aquarius loves to wine and dine and to be courted. Once he finds someone to commit to, he is loyal. In fact, he might even be dependent in his relationships. He rarely feels confined because his mind can easily go off onto another plane when necessary.

In a partnership, the downside of Aquarius is that he is not always focused and has his share of little quirks—he is forgetful and not overly domesticated. The Aquarius female is usually professional and intellectual rather than domestic. Sometimes she has problems recognizing her femininity and seeks constant validation from the men in her life.

DECANS

FIRST DECAN: **Aquarius/Aquarius**—(0 to 10 degrees or approximately January 20–29)

This Aquarius possesses a strong personality and truly marches to the beat of a different drummer. He will have difficulties because he doesn't want to adapt and can be positively pigheaded. While he doesn't need to adapt, he does need to stop working up a resistance just for the sake of resisting.

Aquarius in this decan is an innovator. He can foretell the future. However, if he imposes his insights or lacks the patience and finesse required to share his foresight and wait

for others to accept his ideas, he will become overbearing—
the type that nobody wants to believe or deal with. He is
not going to be understood, which will be lonely and difficult for him.

SECOND DECAN: **Aquarius/Gemini**—(10 to 20 degrees or
approximately January 30–February 8)

The flighty, mercurial quality of Gemini influencing this
decan creates a mind that roams all over the place. This is a
friendly Aquarius who is sociable and active. The Aquarius/
Gemini combination makes him nosy and curious as well
as humanistic and congenial, so it produces a real social
butterfly. This Aquarius can be sent all over the world and
quickly adapt to any place or culture.

THIRD DECAN: **Aquarius/Libra**—(20 to 30 degrees or approximately February 9–18)

Talk about flair! This is the artist who will be doing something at the consciousness-raising level, predicting fashion
or artistic trends, or choosing a color that becomes popular
next year.

If afflicted, this decan of Aquarius can detach emotionally and completely. He will leave you cold, be disinterested,
and have absolutely no desire to empathize. He needs to be
willing to make contact and be vulnerable and unafraid
of his feelings, so instead of detaching, he can make emotional connections with others.

PISCES (FEBRUARY 19–MARCH 20)

Symbol—The Fish

Ruling Planet—Neptune/Jupiter

Element—Water

Cross—Mutable

Group—Theoretical

Gender—Feminine

House Ruled—Twelfth

Famous Pisceans—Rihanna, Albert Einstein, Michelangelo, George Harrison, Elizabeth Taylor, Justin Bieber, Ruth Bader Ginsburg, Steve Jobs, George Washington, Simone Biles

Basic Personality

Pisces occupies the twelfth house and is ruled by Neptune. Because Jupiter ruled this sign in ancient times, Pisces has dual rulership. Jupiter provides intuition while Neptune provides depth, making Pisces the deepest of all constellations.

Pisces is multifaceted and multitalented. It is the ultimate sign with qualities that encompass all signs of the Zodiac. Pisces is intuitive, imaginative, and possesses an insight into human nature that bestows her with compassion and an "others before me" attitude. She is empathetic and people-oriented. As a theoretical sign, Pisces displays, feeds, and expresses her ego through other people. An innate sense of intuition provides her with an awareness of both her abilities and limitations. It enables Pisces to correct her fears so that she doesn't become vague and float out into never-never land.

A dual personality, Pisces is symbolized by two fish swimming in opposite directions. This opposing nature creates a split psyche. This means she can be a medium—Pisces can detach so that she can tap into someone else's ego. She retains her identity while empathizing with others. At a positive level, this is wonderful because it gives Pisces psychic ability. She can think in the abstract and go beyond the boundaries and limitations of all the other Sun Signs. On the negative side, Neptune makes Pisces unpredictable and difficult to understand. Her irrational fears can make her phobic. However, her chameleon quality allows her to withstand anything—she has the key to survival. On the other hand, it often handicaps Pisces because unless she develops self-awareness and learns how to appreciate her intuitive and psychic abilities, she will doubt them. To counter this, Pisces must learn to use and depend on her gut.

Pisces picks up the vibrations of others. As a result, she often projects not only her own problems but also the problems of those around her. This can be mentally and emotionally draining, so periodic isolation is healthy and vital for Pisces—she needs to eliminate all stimulation and recuperate. When consumed by severe fear or anger, she can move away from people and isolate. Meditation can be helpful to Pisces when all else has failed.

Although Pisces needs solitude, she fears being alone. She sometimes develops a need to please others for fear of being rejected. When negatively afflicted, or when frightened and uncertain, Pisces suffers terribly from the what-ifs. This makes it difficult for her to deal with *what is*. She can become a loner or dependent and insecure. It's dangerous when Pisces starts depending on others for motivation or validation—she gets limited and nasty and, consequently, vindictive.

When afflicted, Pisces is lazy, vague, and lacks concentration. She can become overly emotional to the point of hysteria—in Pisces, hysteria abounds when she is in doubt, afraid, or uncertain. She will become bad-tempered and self-indulgent without boundaries. Pisces will hang on to imaginary hurts and misinterpret things. She will go to any length to satisfy her ego, becoming deceitful if need be. The self-indulgence of Pisces can reach epic proportions. When this occurs, she must get her central nervous system back into a relaxed state; otherwise, there will be adverse effects on her health.

Pisces is quick to jump to conclusions, so she must learn to hold judgment until her intuition proves the right or wrong of a situation. This way, she can relate to others without blaming or taking things personally. When this intuition is used as a self-disciplining device, Pisces is powerful and can accomplish a great deal.

With education, self-awareness, and strength, Pisces can be creative, artistic, and productive. The responsibility of Pisces is to do the right kind of juggling act where she can have a free flow back and forth between the abstract and the concrete. This will enable her to tap into others and make use of her instincts and ideas.

Talents and Abilities

Pisces is a multitalented sign. She can make strides in the world of medicine, especially as a diagnostician or psychologist. Because she has visualization and an innate understanding and absorption of others' egos, Pisces makes a great actor who can take on any role—be anything, do anything.

Pisces also has a keen sense of humor and could be a good comedian.

As talented as Pisces is, she also has a lazy streak. She wants others to do it for her. She thinks she is subtle. Suggestions abound, even when she is not willing to do the work. Pisces must learn that "doing it yourself" is the only way to master. She must learn to strike a balance between laziness and industriousness and to focus her talents and master something.

Health and Physical Traits

Pisces rules the feet and all the filtration glands.

Physically, Pisces is not strong. Most of her health problems are central nervous system related. Since Pisces must learn to overcome dependency, fear, and rejection, internal struggles are exhausting. Regeneration is instrumental to the health and well-being of Pisces. She must take periodic breaks to relax and reenergize.

Family Relationships

As a mother-dominated sign, Pisces tends to pick up on and imitate Mother—good, bad, or indifferent. Mother is instrumental to Pisces, while Father is a fantasy. It takes a long time for a Pisces to understand her father, if he is there at all. It is hard for a Pisces to know her father and vice versa. She has a crossed perception of Dad that is oddly shaped by her mother's definition, her father's actions (or inactions), and the truth. But it takes a while to get the truth. Neptune doesn't allow for clarity, making it hard for Pisces to know who her father is and where he fits in. This usually does not occur until later in life. If there is a relationship with Dad, Pisces will bend over backward to please him.

The Pisces mother, like the other theoretical signs, is poor. Pisces tends to lack the consistency needed to rear a child with the great security that all children need. She can become a martyr, making her children feel guilty— that if she cares for her children, they owe her. The Pisces mother can be industrious and dutiful, particularly if her own mother was that way. But if her mother was lazy and disorganized, Pisces will manifest those traits.

The Pisces father is lazy. He can live vicariously through his offspring, which causes the child to fight for his identity because the father is either projecting or rejecting his parental responsibility altogether.

The Pisces child has a complex emotional life. The underlying problem is that she is conscious of the family and is sensitive—she picks up everybody's vibrations. She transcends her age in terms of this understanding but is helpless to do anything about it. When this becomes overwhelming or overstimulating, it causes her to withdraw. She escapes into fantasy or television. It is helpful for the Pisces child to keep busy and active so that she doesn't isolate and brood. The imagination of the Pisces child can blossom into something creative and positive for her development and growth.

Partnerships

If Pisces emulates Mother or can't let go of Mother's impact, she will bring those characteristics to her partnerships. Pisces will have opinions about partners, particularly about men, based on her mother's perceptions. For the Pisces man, if he finds he can't treat, act, or have his partner behave like his mother, there will be relationship difficulties. Pisces needs to be intelligent and flexible enough to recognize that his mate is his or her own person.

The Pisces female often succumbs to her husband's demands. When she doesn't want to do this, she will do what is requested in appearance only, then turn around and undermine her spouse. She can become sneaky.

Since she has an emotional personality, Pisces will often marry and wrap herself around a partner. Pisces is superficially dependent—she uses dependency as a control issue. She must stop trying to get her partner to do what she thinks her partner should do. When Pisces develops positively, she will realize that her security does not depend on controlling circumstances or other people. She needs to be careful of control, even though it is not done overtly.

Although romantic, Pisces is not overly passionate and sometimes feels sex is a duty. She assumes that romance is all that is necessary for a relationship. Pisces's inherent loneliness can be overcome by taking a leap of faith and turning to spirituality, rather than a mate, for security and strength. If Pisces finds and develops strength, she will discover that she actually has more to offer than her mate.

DECANS

FIRST DECAN: **Pisces/Pisces**—(0 to 10 degrees or approximately February 19–29)

Neptune can be frightening, so Pisces in the first decan has a great deal to resolve. She must control the depth of her water quality and accept that no one else will feel this level of emotion. While it may appear to be a lonely trip, the result is enlightening. Pisces will eventually reach a point where she is not alone. This will happen when she can touch her soul or reach a spirituality of sorts. When this occurs, Pisces will recognize and be able to deal with her emotional depth, unite with the universe, and cease to feel lonely. The enlightenment is a source of power that allows Pisces to become securer.

If afflicted, Pisces will brood and feel sorry for herself or be overcome with either irrational fear of the unknown (which can relate to past lives) or the what-ifs. Although obsessing over the what-ifs prevents her from fully enjoying the present, Pisces does this to overcome karma—the twelfth house, which Pisces rules.

SECOND DECAN: **Pisces/Cancer**—(10 to 20 degrees or approximately March 1–10)

This is perhaps the most difficult of the three decans. The Cancer/Moon instability, coupled with Neptune's fear, can make for a moody, unhappy, self-pitying individual. Pisces must learn to harden and to have faith—it will help her move on with her life and goals. Without these tools, Pisces will become immobilized, afraid to take the next step because she is convinced the worst is going to happen. Pisces can reach the ultimate heights or the lowest of depths, depending on where her Moon takes her and what other afflictions or strengths may be revealed in the natal chart.

This decan needs to get out of herself and do something for someone else—if too self-absorbed, it tires her system and takes its toll on her health.

THIRD DECAN: **Pisces/Scorpio**—(20 to 30 degrees or approximately March 11–20)

Since Scorpio is always strong, this decan of Pisces also has the good fortune of being strong. The glitch here is that Scorpio brings an intensity that makes Pisces either very good or very bad—if Pisces is very good, she is phenomenal, but if she's very bad, she will be selfish, destructive, and narcissistic. She will use her strength as a self-serving tool that will most certainly prove to be her undoing. On the other hand, if positive, Pisces can share her strength with others and serve. As she serves others, she becomes more dynamic and attractive.

Sun Through the Houses

Once you become familiar with your Sun Sign, you're going to find that it isn't always in its natural house. The Sun Sign of Aries doesn't always fall in the Aries-ruled first house, the Sun Sign of Taurus doesn't always land in the Taurus-ruled second house, and so on. It is purely dependent on your hour of birth and the rising sign (ascendant). Your rising sign is always in the first house, and it determines the placement of all your planets in their respective houses.

SUN IN THE FIRST HOUSE

When the Sun is occupying the first house, it becomes "head-on." This means it must experience, it must do. It takes on youthful, courageous, and enthusiastic qualities. In the first house, the Sun will be driven and will often jump without thinking.

If afflicted, this active, energetic quality turns into arrogance, which is nothing more than a cover for fear. The ego becomes stifled—sneaky on some occasions, bombastic on others. There is a tendency to overcompensate, to justify and explain itself, feeling as if it is not quite sure it has a right to be, due to an innate fear of rejection.

SUN IN THE SECOND HOUSE

The Sun desires anything material in nature. There is a need to develop the financial power necessary to obtain all the luxury, beauty, and possessions that this Venus-ruled house demands.

If afflicted, financial and material resources may be squandered. Although there is a natural grace in earning money, it will usually slip right through the fingers, sometimes through gambling. An affliction can either create laziness or the tendency to take things for granted.

SUN IN THE THIRD HOUSE

The Sun in this house needs to express the self and be understood. It prompts a desire to be educated in ways that enhance both self-awareness and self-expression. A talent for communicating is apparent in this house, whether through writing, teaching, public speaking, or painting. If afflicted, the need for education and self-expression could lead to chattiness and intellectual snobbery.

SUN IN THE FOURTH HOUSE

The Sun in this placement is going to be a nurturer. It is self-protecting and self-sustaining and needs to connect with the self. The Sun in this placement also has an innate need to amass and cling to possessions, feeling unstable and uncertain about its lot.

When afflicted, Sun in the fourth house is someone who doesn't want to leave home. This is the thirty-five-year-old bachelor (or bachelorette) whom Mom is still looking after because he craves the comfort and protection of home or is afraid to leave. This is also the type of person who, in a divorce case, would rather kill than lose possession of the house.

SUN IN THE FIFTH HOUSE

This is a powerful placement because the Sun is in domicile position in this house. No matter how weak the rest of a chart may be, with the Sun placed in the fifth house, the individual takes on a creative quality, performs without fear, and has a desire to express and accomplish.

A person with this placement seldom strays from a spouse or family. It is not his or her forte—he is honest and generally cannot handle more than one partner. Men with the Sun in this placement make devoted, affectionate, and committed fathers, even to the point of competing with their wives.

Should it be afflicted, unfortunately, this is going to bring about a great deal of difficulty in these same areas. The individual might become unstable and wander. A father might either neglect his children or become so afraid of losing them that he becomes too possessive.

SUN IN THE SIXTH HOUSE

This is a plain old workaholic who just wants to improve and do. He tends to be a loner. If afflicted, he doesn't know how to interact with the world at large. He will find himself exhausted by other people, which will consequently impact his central nervous system. He will frequently have to isolate himself so that he can regenerate.

In health matters, this Sun is not strong and has a low vitality that will need to be compensated for.

SUN IN THE SEVENTH HOUSE

When someone has a Sun placed here, he is considered a "much married" person who always thinks in terms of "we." This person often surrenders his power to his partner. He doesn't realize he's giving his power away—he thinks that the partner is taking it and not being considerate. He doesn't feel he can operate without a partner and feels incomplete and, eventually, frustrated.

The individual with the Sun in this house needs to understand this dynamic and try to function on his own so that he comes to discover himself as a whole person.

SUN IN THE EIGHTH HOUSE

When a person has a Sun in this placement, his life might be tainted by death, whether it be a heart attack that he survives, a near-death experience, or the deaths of people who are important to him. When these losses occur, he must pick up and regenerate and, eventually, let go. This letting go can feel like a death itself, but from this process comes the ability to survive and experience "rebirth."

As a result, this placement is often influential to those whose careers are associated with death—hospice work, undertakers, funeral directors, and the like.

SUN IN THE NINTH HOUSE

The Sun placed here brings forth a natural ability to tap past-life knowledge and religion associated with philosophy, higher learning, and the expansion of the mind. This individual is usually much wiser than his education would denote.

If afflicted or under hardship, this philosophical, abstract quality turns into defiance, creating an individual who might suffer from wanderlust—he wants to be here, there, and everywhere but winds up nowhere.

A person with this placement has a great desire for adventure, travel, and knowledge.

SUN IN THE TENTH HOUSE

This placement indicates someone who will be before the public, someone who will have his fifteen minutes of fame at the very least. This is the house of power, and it produces an individual who works hard for prestige, achievement, and notoriety.

When afflicted, this placement creates an authoritative and dictatorial individual who is certain that his direction is the only way to go. He could wind up being on the lunatic fringe or in a cult or outside of regular government—definitely someone looking to be noticed.

SUN IN THE ELEVENTH HOUSE

This Sun has a lot of hopes and wishes all his own. This is the house of friendship, but a person with this placement needs to be conscious not to spread himself so thin that he loses the ability to identify with anyone or anything in particular. Although the Sun in this house is always friendly, group-oriented, and a humanitarian with the world at large, he is also always on a continuous quest for his own identity.

If afflicted, the Sun in this house is going to get into the habit of rebelling just for the hell of it. He'll break down every order and be unconventional for the sake of being unconventional. He can be eccentric and odd.

SUN IN THE TWELFTH HOUSE

This Sun is mysterious. The twelfth house is the reservoir of wonderful past-life abilities, talents, and techniques. Yet when the Sun is placed here, the misfortune is that the individual has a sensation of confinement. And often, he is confined. It can be a complete confinement such as a wheelchair or a jail term, or confinement through one's inner fears and limitations.

In this house, the Sun also experiences transmutation. The individual begins to slow down and listen. It might require a Saturn or Jupiter transit over the Sun to reveal that this confinement or limitation doesn't exist; it is usually self-imposed. The individual can go from feeling confined to listening to his subconscious. This allows him to flower. Talents emerge, perhaps some he never knew existed. This is the house where limitations can be transcended, and with transcendence comes liberation.

5

Ascendants—
Your Rising Sign

The ascendant, or rising sign, indicates how you see yourself. The position of your rising sign in relationship to your Sun and your Moon defines your unique personality. The rising sign is the third leg of this astrological trilogy—Sun, Moon, and ascendant—which represents your id, your conscience, and your superego.

The rising sign is your future. It acts as a protective layer, shielding your Sun and Moon Signs, so that they can develop. You are always your Sun Sign and Moon Sign, but the ascendant sign represents the socialization process. When integrated with the Sun and Moon, one is whole. Your rising sign is the part of your personality that is not going to leave you wide open, available to anybody's pot-shots or concepts and ideas. The rising sign is your best foot forward, the fashion in which you operate. It is who you let the world think you are.

As Earth rotates every twenty-four hours, it brings a new rising sign on the horizon approximately every two hours.

Whatever sign was on the horizon at your exact time of birth becomes your rising sign. It also determines where your first house is placed (and in what sign). Your rising sign is always in the first house of your birth chart on the eastern horizon.

ARIES RISING

The emotional sign of Aries represents the ego. The simplest equation for a healthy ego is knowing what you want and feeling you deserve it. In the case of Aries rising, when that is achieved, he is at peace. When it is not, he winds up getting pushy, overbearing, and prone to temper tantrums. No matter how elevated the Sun Sign, an Aries rising needs to develop moderation; otherwise, his friends or partners will walk away, leaving him to wonder, "What did I do?"

Aries rising is materialistic. He is not religiously or philosophically inclined. The aggressive and impulsive Martian quality of Aries gives him physical and sexual energy. If Aries rising learns to sublimate this energy, there is no limit to what he can do. This is raw and crude energy that must be channeled positively and productively, and accomplished through dancing, martial arts, sports, or crafts. Without any kind of discipline or direction, this energy of Mars will lead to difficulty and conflict with other people.

Youngsters with Aries rising can find themselves in accidents. These are children who have no foresight or fear of consequences. They need to be guided. Once guided and disciplined, that energy can be redirected into a more positive and structured quality to avoid the symbolic ramming of the horns against the wall.

Many successful people with this rising sign have careers and achievements associated with any number of things you find in the Aries Sun Sign, such as acting or the military. Aries rising is quick and intelligent.

TAURUS RISING

Taurus is ruled by Venus, and Venus filters out that which is crude to produce refinement. This will make Taurus rising appear placid and an easygoing pushover.

Taurus rising is emotional. She is also slow and deliberate. Once she puts her hooves in, she will follow through and act, no matter what. But she must do it at her own pace—with any kind of prodding, pushing, or disturbance of her equilibrium, she is going to flare up like a bull.

Taurus rising has a natural affinity to all things that are lovely and refined. She likes good food, good wine, and good living conditions. She wants a comfortable, pleasurable, and enjoyable lifestyle and environment—and she'll work for it, too. She possesses an energy and a love for labor that is endless.

Family and community-oriented, Taurus rising will make sure that her children go to the best schools and live in the best home in the best community. She is very conscious of who the neighbors are and how she lives within her home. She wants a lovely environment and will put a lot of energy into making her home beautiful. If she loses her equilibrium, she will get depressed if anything around her is dirty or does not live up to her high standards.

Sometimes Taurus rising needs to prove herself over and over. It is a tedious, heartbreaking, and energy-consuming position that will eventually lead poor old Taurus rising to feel as though her efforts are of little use. When this happens, she begins to get negative, lazy, and unkempt until inertia takes over, causing her to negate her positive qualities and strengths. As in the Taurus Sun Sign, Taurus rising doesn't want to display her temper. She is afraid that her temper will disturb her equilibrium and refined Venus quality. To avoid conflict, she holds in and stockpiles her anger. But one day, when there is no more to be taken, the dam breaks and the bull charges.

This rising sign needs a great deal of physical affection—her five senses are keen, particularly touch. Taurus rising needs a lot of stroking and cuddling. As a baby, she's the one who'll want to sleep with her parents; as an adult, she can't walk in or out the door without kissing everybody.

GEMINI RISING

Gemini has a dual nature, and on the rising sign, that mercurial quality is going to show up immediately. Gemini rising is fickle. He is doing a balancing act and can't afford to deal with everything as though it were going to be a career, so he touches and gathers here, picks a brain over there, and accumulates enough information to keep on going without staying in one place for too long.

Although Gemini rising is optimistic and quick of mind, he should make sure that his thoughts and feelings are in unison to become a better communicator. He must learn to be consistent so that he doesn't have difficulties with a partner. If he says one thing now and the opposite three hours later, his partner will perceive him as a liar and problems will ensue.

In a positive light, Gemini rising has mental agility, allowing him to excel in any form of writing, music, or even politics. Many individuals with this ascendant have achieved fame and success. If negative, Gemini rising can be nothing more than a gossip. He can play games, the most common of which is that, when you are intellectual with him, he is emotional, and vice versa. Worst of all, once he makes you lose your equilibrium or temper, he'll get very cold-blooded.

Gemini rising is quick and intellectual, with a great deal of retained knowledge and a good head for trivia. The downside is that he can also lack the depth to sustain any train of thought or action—he goes from one idea to the next. Gemini rising needs to master something or else he'll become a jack-of-all-trades and master of none.

Gemini rising works well in combination with a fixed Sun Sign, such as Taurus, Leo, Scorpio, or Aquarius, because it allows a fixed sign to see both sides of the coin.

CANCER RISING

Cancer rising is emotional and sentimental, sensitive, nurturing, and protective—the type who draws others to her.

Since the rising sign protects the rest of the chart, and the Moon is the ruler of Cancer rising, it creates the appearance of vulnerability. When Cancer rising feels her vulnerability is not at risk, she is forthcoming. But should she feel any kind of threat, she will batten down the hatches, tighten up like a crab, and submerge. That vulnerability will turn to moodiness.

Cancer rising is always ready to get going. She likes to get things organized, to ensure the comfort of the home and the comfort of the self. She makes collecting an art form. If afflicted, Cancer rising will hold on to material possessions above all else. She has a morbid fear of losing, so she is always collecting or initiating. As noted in the Sun Sign, Cancer is the polarity of starvation, so this innate fear of loss is manifested by hoarding and hanging on to everything because she is afraid of the inability to replace. Look in the basement of any Cancer rising and there will be a lifetime of memorabilia and artifacts.

The sensitivity of Cancer rising can lead to self-pity. There is nobody like a Cancer to feel sorry for herself—she thinks she is being taken advantage of. As a result, she develops defense mechanisms—she gets prickly, overly annoyed, and touchy and can become extremely bitter and resentful.

Most difficulties of Cancer rising come from a need for emotional fortification. The misfortune of this is that when Cancer rising begins to feel sorry for herself, even if the reasons are legitimate, she begins to stroke her ego in a dangerous way, sometimes by escaping through drugs or alcohol.

In a positive light, Cancer rising can be very effective. Her intense emotions make her an excellent actor or successful in the arts. She can also provide a great deal of aid and comfort to others, tending to the sick and nurturing those who are less fortunate. In fact, giving her emotions away to benefit others is not only healthy for Cancer rising but can also lead to a worthwhile vocation and a great deal of success.

LEO RISING

When Leo is rising, it personifies the image of a lion strutting with power. The Sun rules Leo rising and gives it a vitality and a dynamic personality. He radiates a sunny disposition, a magnetism, especially in the male (the female is also magnetic but, through no fault of her own, tends to draw envy). Powerful individuals will be drawn to the magnetic personality of Leo rising. As such, it almost guarantees that Leo rising will be an executive or in a position that puts him among people where leadership and executive abilities are important. Leo rising has the ability to make money.

By nature, Leo rising is easygoing. He loves color, has a certain flair, and excellent taste. He enjoys pomp and circumstance, ceremonies, and uniforms. He relishes dressing up and being singled out from the rest. While he might dress in a black suit, he'll wear an outrageous tie just to be different—he aims to get attention. However, if this royal, magnificent animal is afflicted, what you get is a downright broken ego, which leads to sloppiness and a lack of self-esteem and self-respect. Once that happens, Leo becomes disrespectful. Drama is part of the Leo Sun, Moon, and rising sign. He can be capable and exceptionally talented or, in the negative sense, take everything that happens and turn it into melodrama.

If afflicted, Leo rising can have a bad temper, display bossiness, and be susceptible to flattery. An old saying goes, "Flattery is like perfume—you sniff it, but you never swallow it." Leo rising must take heed because he can be manipulated and victimized by this vulnerability. But if he is fully aware of his abilities and strength, he can't be pushed or led by adulation.

Leo rising will never forget a favor. He has a long memory, so anyone who is kind, helpful, or trustworthy will wind up in the longest-term friendship imaginable. The misfortune of a betrayed Leo rising is that an injury to his ego will never be forgotten. Even if he has to deal with you, work with you, or be your companion, he will never trust you again.

VIRGO RISING

Virgo rising is a bit of a loner. She tires of people since they distract her focus and drain her energy. Virgo rising loves labor and enjoys being alone. She doesn't want anyone hovering over her watching what she does. Ruled by Mercury, she is intelligent and a veritable workhorse. Virgo rising is not bored by details, and contentedly nitpicks, going through all the little mundane pieces that support major projects. She is like an accountant who locates that missing penny with great satisfaction.

Virgo rising has a curious mind. She learns things and stores away all this treasured information knowing that, sooner or later, when she has to find an answer or come up with some ingenious solution, she can tap into this valuable resource in the back of her head. As in the Virgo Sun Sign, she has an enormous ability for self-analysis, which can help her deal with her shortcomings.

If afflicted, Virgo rising will clean the stove until it shines but forgets the sink and the rest of the kitchen. She gets too bogged down with perfecting the details so that other things wind up going to pot. Virgo rising is so busy breaking apart and taking care of segments that she often misses the big picture. She can be nitpicky, critical, condemning, or otherwise get herself into trouble.

What Virgo rising needs most is approval. Unfortunately, her background is usually one in which she draws criticism, so that, somewhere along the line, she will have to distinguish between being analyzed and being criticized, which, of course, are two very different things. Virgo rising doesn't handle criticism well, but she's awfully good at dishing it out. She is looking for perfection, but perfection, like beauty, is in the eye of the beholder. She needs to be more open and accepting of other people's flaws.

LIBRA RISING

Libra is ruled by the planet Venus, which endows Libra rising with a natural grace and beauty. The beauty that comes from Libra/Venus is a balanced beauty of both face and body.

Libra rising is concerned not only with graciousness and diplomacy but with stability. He needs to stabilize and be in complete command of his mental faculties. To maintain equilibrium, Libra rising needs to remove himself from anything that is nerve-racking—stress, tension, or pressure—because he doesn't handle it well.

To be in perfect balance is Libra rising's life quest. Out of that comes a strength and ability to detach and be non-judgmental. Like the Libra Sun Sign, Libra rising can look at a situation and be an excellent judge because he can see both sides of the coin, offer pure objectivity, and come to a fair and equitable conclusion. That's a rare gift that is not bestowed on other signs.

If afflicted, Libra rising won't give a damn. This detachment is incredible because, although he will appear to be caring, underneath there won't be even a drop of concern. In matters of diplomacy, when it is necessary to speak and act cordially without a single emotion attached to it, this can be a formidable quality. But in personal relationships, it is nothing but trouble because a friend or mate will be looking to get a reaction and Libra rising will remain frustratingly cool, balanced, and unresponsive.

Venus rules everything that is artistic, beautifying, or that satisfies the senses. People with Libra rising are usually successful in any creative field—fashion design, art, acting, interior decorating, and the like.

Women and men with Libra rising have an overall physical attractiveness due to the symmetry of their bodies and facial features. It is the type of beauty that is everlasting.

SCORPIO RISING

When Scorpio is rising, it creates a strong personality that you either love or hate—there is no in-between. Scorpio rising, like the Scorpio Sun Sign, is an extremist. She can possess enormous magnetism or create repulsion. She can be either an absolute darling or the most hateful individual—when she's good, she's very good, but when she's bad, she's awful.

Scorpio rising readily sorts out who is worthy in her life

and whom she will annihilate. Her energies flow without guilt, and she doesn't care whether you like her or not. If you like her, all the better, but if you don't, it's of little consequence. This attitude makes her stone-faced and austere in appearance. Her eyes are piercing, but they can also intimidate—they either send a message to stay away or they'll look right through you. They are eyes that can mesmerize you.

Scorpio risings are magnetic. They exude psychic, sexual energy that flows freely and is attractive. If a Scorpio rising doesn't realize that she has this power, she will likely misuse it.

Scorpio is ruled by Pluto, which deals with the underworld. When afflicted, it can lead Scorpio rising into a controversial lifestyle and mischievous dealings that might eventually have her wind up where she least expects it—in jail or even dead—if she's not careful.

Positively, Scorpio rising's powerful energy can lead and influence large groups of people. If she dedicates herself to the service or welfare of others, she will become a formidable individual.

SAGITTARIUS RISING

Sagittarius rising has an uncanny ability to bend the will of the universe to serve him. This willful, broad-minded, and intuitive personality can attract and acquire financial security without thinking twice. On the other hand, if negatively aspected, he will develop a dangerous and narcissistic attitude that begins to take things for granted, believing he can have anything he wants.

Freewheeling, curious, elegant, and friendly, Sagittarius rising is charming, pleasant, talkative, and generous. Yet he's also extraordinarily fickle. When he gets bored and tired, he cuts fast. He wants to be challenged, and if you don't challenge him, he'll move on to somebody else who can. Sagittarius rising desires respect and approval, but that's hard to come by for somebody who doesn't always stick around.

A female with Sagittarius rising seeks approval from her father and, if it is not forthcoming, will work to get approval from other males. She doesn't have it easy—femininity doesn't always come naturally to her.

A male with this rising sign gets bored easily and wants to move on. This gets him in trouble, especially if he's married, since he usually considers that his wife—not he—is the one who's married, giving him carte blanche to do his own thing.

When afflicted, Sagittarius rising gets sloppy and stops dressing well. He also gets unconcerned about feelings—others' and his own—and begins a downward, negative streak where he expects perfection from others even when he is less than perfect or unable to cope.

Sagittarius rising is freedom-loving and doesn't like to be fenced in. When he starts feeling confined, either physically or emotionally, it takes its toll. He needs to work hard to transcend this condition or he will certainly pay the consequences.

CAPRICORN RISING

Whereas most rising signs share the characteristics of their Sun Sign counterparts, Capricorn rising is a bit of an anomaly. A Capricorn Sun is usually tall and extroverted, but on the rising sign, she is short and a little cool and aloof. It's a strange phenomenon, but Saturn's impact on the rising sign diminishes and takes certain things away.

Capricorn rising is more involved with the maturation of the ego than the Sun Sign since the first house / ascendant house is the house of the ego. Some Capricorn risings look and act old in their youth—they're six-year-old little old men and women. They're sweet yet cautious, as though they have knowledge and awareness that belies their age. However, the older they get, the better they get. As Capricorn rising matures, instead of remaining a little old lady, the child inside finally begins to emerge; she starts to look and act youthful and develops a wonderful sense of humor. A sixty-year-old Capricorn rising sometimes looks younger and better than a forty-year-old. As she gets older, Capricorn rising gains a sense of freedom because she has already taken care of all her responsibilities and can simply begin to enjoy life at last.

If afflicted, Capricorn rising loses her self-control and

high responsibility level. She can also lead a double life. Although a conservative and respectable individual to those around her, when she leaves town, she really lets down her hair and loosens up. As an earth sign, Capricorn rising has a sensuality and a passion that she keeps hidden under the weight of maturity and responsibility because she is afraid of being judged. She won't do anything that she feels violates her code of ethics in her immediate environment—she'll just do it out of town.

Capricorn rising doesn't want to recognize her ego and puts a brick wall around it. When she can't get past that brick wall to give out and receive the companionship and love she craves, she gets frustrated, tense, and, eventually, ill.

Capricorn rising creates tension because she has to be in control, has to do it herself, and feels that nobody else can be trusted to do it as well as she can. This control issue leads to such symptoms as migraine headaches, sleeping disorders, and teeth grinding. She's got to let it go and start having faith in the abilities of others.

Capricorn rising needs to be the savior of her family and friends. She is often an enabler as well. Everybody benefits because a Capricorn rising boss will employ everyone she knows, feeling as if she's the only one who can provide support and guidance. If afflicted, this need to have everyone under one roof will be done for the sake of control and manipulation. Sooner or later, this is going to backfire, which will lead to difficult confrontations. If Capricorn rising finds dissension, disloyalty, or loss of control, she will revert to the one thing she can control—pouring every bit of her energy into work and earning money. She will become the ultimate workaholic. Sadly, this is often triggered by the fact that she doesn't feel loved. She begins to believe that if she works hard and produces more, she'll be well liked. Unfortunately, what happens is that Capricorn rising only winds up feeling betrayed.

During the Aquarian Age, Capricorn risings are likely to see the value of their serious and philosophical concepts and wind up earning their livings in New Age fields such as astrology, yoga, and the metaphysical sciences.

AQUARIUS RISING

Aquarius is ruled by Uranus, the planet of eccentricity, giving Aquarius rising a unique personality. Uranus demands that you identify yourself with and retain your individuality. Early in life, the child with Aquarius rising is going to be labeled *precocious*. This child knows precisely what he wants. However, if there is an affliction, he will lack identity and do whatever his friends are doing.

With maturity, the electricity of the Aquarius rising personality comes forth and begins to attract. It takes creativity and work to get and keep the attention of an Aquarius rising—his mind wanders, so you need to be quick, get to the point, or shock him—or you will lose him.

Aquarius rising needs mental freedom. He's a natural storyteller. As a child, he possesses a great imagination and will make up little stories and fantasies. Sometimes he is even falsely accused of lying. He is not lying but merely creating, and he innately knows the difference. If afflicted, he can become a child who, because he lacks identity, doesn't know where he stands or can't relate to his environment, and this will prompt him to speak in half-truths or lies.

The Aquarius rising personality is often misunderstood. He's not easy to understand or accept because of an innate ability to transcend the mundane. An Aquarius rising is out of step with society, sometimes even ahead of it. How can he fit in? Sometimes, he needs to quiet down his personality and wait for the rest of the world to catch up.

Aquarius rising is prophetic—he can look ahead and see the result of a situation. If he is not honed or polished, he can wind up becoming indiscreet, putting his foot in his mouth, and getting into trouble because of the prematurity of his thoughts and actions.

Aquarius rising is a humanitarian who is friendly and well liked. He is happy, entertaining, and enjoys being part of a group. If afflicted, he becomes rebellious and will destroy the status quo just for the heck of it. He will love uprooting traditions and making sure that everyone around him is uncomfortable with what is going on. He'll even set up an argument just to be on the other side of it and create controversy. Although he is wise, intelligent, and ahead of his time, if not careful, he'll wind up running ahead and jumping over the edge.

PISCES RISING

Pisces rising is difficult to decipher. Neptune, the ruler of Pisces, can create an individual with an impenetrable façade, the world's finest actor, and the chameleon of the universe. This can be hugely misleading. Pisces is a water sign, the ultimate of water signs, possessing the most exceptional psychic ability bestowed on any of the constellations.

Pisces rising has a big problem—early in life, she begins picking up the vibes of her surroundings and the emotions of other people. This is problematic because she then has difficulty separating her personal energy from that of others. As a result, she is filled continuously with strange sensations that must be separated and put into proper perspective.

An idealist, Pisces rising sees things through rose-colored glasses, giving everyone the benefit of the doubt. Her idealism is frequently crushed when she must face the reality of other people's faults and frailties. She expects others to live up to her expectations, puts people on pedestals, expects the very best, and almost always winds up being crushed. The irony here is that while Pisces rising innately understands the reality of others' limitations, she prefers to be romantic and idealistic.

If afflicted, Pisces rising is enormously lazy, never getting up off her butt and doing what needs to get done. This is a shame because she is multitalented. When well-aspected, Pisces rising is successful and resourceful—if she can't earn a living one way, she'll earn it in another.

Mood swings are also common to Pisces rising. One moment she's happy, exuding a positiveness to those around her, and the next moment she's falling into a depression, feeling sorry for herself or accusing others of illusionary things that don't exist—or do! Pisces rising can swing between these extreme highs and lows to the point where she loses energy and becomes dependent, moody, demanding, overbearing, and, most of all, afraid.

Pisces rising is psychic. She can pick up on truths that others are trying to hide. However, she must learn to wait, for truths do eventually surface and prove her correct. Pisces must also learn to trust. In doing so, her mood swings will diminish.

It is advisable for Pisces rising to find an outlet, whether it be through religion or medicine—anything that benefits others. Sooner or later, Pisces rising must serve and share. If she doesn't, she will wind up submerged in her own misery, drowning in those waters of emotion that cannot serve anyone, including herself. As such, she is like a sponge that has absorbed much too much water and must be squeezed to get rid of the overflow. As she gives of herself to others, Pisces rising becomes stronger and functions more productively.

Pisces rising's strength lies in believing what she knows to be true, even if others are in denial. Time can be her best ally when she trusts her inner knowledge.

6

Planets Through the Signs and Houses

MOON

The Moon represents the Mother. Mother is your inheritance factor, the underbelly, representing your subconscious motivations, which can often prevent you from connecting with your emotions. Emotional maturity allows the qualities of the Moon to integrate with the Sun. The Moon has no light of its own; it reflects the Sun.

The Moon takes approximately twenty-nine days to revolve around Earth, spending two to three days in each constellation. The Moon rules the sign of Cancer and the fourth house, which is the entrance of the soul.

The Moon also represents your body. The Moon and its aspects will influence what you look like, your health, and how you will respond emotionally to the world around you.

Moon Through the Signs

MOON IN ARIES

With a Moon in Aries, there is the potential for danger. The Moon is the vehicle by which emotion is felt and displayed, and so its placement in this fire sign makes Moon in Aries impulsive. He has a quick temper and often takes things too personally, responding in a reactionary way without thinking. This spontaneity of rage can be foolhardy, exploding like a firecracker. When Moon in Aries senses the slightest intimidation, he will react and hit before he gets hit. After he's cooled off, he might be sorry and ask for forgiveness, but one thing is guaranteed—it will happen over and over again.

MOON IN TAURUS

The Moon in Taurus can hold rages so long and intensely that one day he'll simply blow up. Moon in Taurus doesn't know how to handle emotions well and must learn to deal with each indignation as it comes up rather than stockpiling them.

Far more than other signs, Moon in Taurus has an enormous interest in money. His emotional security is dependent on finances. Moon in Taurus is hardworking and possesses stamina, physical agility, and an energy that makes for a good earner—he's persistent and will stay there long after everybody else has quit. Financial security provides Moon in Taurus with the ability to enjoy the "good life" he so innately desires.

The emotions of Moon in Taurus are passionate and intense. When well-aspected, he is charming, loves beautiful things, and is sensitive to his surroundings. He has a sexual attractiveness that can belie his physical appearance. Both males and females with Moon in Taurus have a sexual magnetism that attract others. Until you sting a Moon in Taurus, you don't know how ferocious he can be.

MOON IN GEMINI

Moon in Gemini must work hard for stability because it doesn't come naturally. He is prone to bursts of nervous energy, and his mind and body are in constant conflict— the body contains emotions when emotions are there to be felt. Moon in Gemini doesn't want to feel, he wants to intellectualize, and so he is caught between the rational and the emotional. Because of this mind-body conflict, Moon in Gemini winds up exhausted. When afflicted, this can be unhealthy and lead to illness.

Moon in Gemini needs to enhance his mind-over-body control through focus, study, and developing self-awareness. Without this, he might self-destruct.

MOON IN CANCER

Moon in Cancer mothers the world and has psychic ability. But Moon in Cancer is also oversensitive, moody, and emotional. He can be easygoing, sociable, and entertaining, but he first needs to be flattered, stroked, and appreciated.

Moon in Cancer is friendly but can also be touchy and prickly. This is a spiteful Moon if afflicted—one that will not forget hurts but just move away and snub you. The Moon in Cancer takes everything personally, often without thinking. He will begin to amass possessions as a way of compensating for his emotional voids.

MOON IN LEO

The Moon in Leo is strong and has a natural agility, energy, and vitality not found anywhere else. His need for prominence—the desire to be noticed—translates into a flair. When he cooks, he cooks with a flair; when he designs, he designs with a flair—even if he's making a bed, he'll do that with a flair, too. He is creative and powerful. Moon in Leo is like that regal lion taking care of his den—he'll proudly roam around his domain, making sure everyone is safe.

Moon in Leo is an idealist. Wealth only comes to Leo when he can adjust to the reality of his environment and his source of income. Nothing is as strange or devastating to a Leo as how he earns a living. Money is far more important than he lets on.

If afflicted, since Leo rules the heart, Moon in Leo can be prone to heart conditions. This is a manifestation of his disappointment in his ability to achieve his preconceived level of status.

MOON IN VIRGO

The Moon in Virgo is an isolated and reserved individual. Even when among others, he is usually quiet. He harbors an inferiority complex, and when that begins to surface, he withdraws emotion and becomes analytical and critical, putting up a cold façade. If you prod, push, or burden him in any way, he's going to respond nastily.

Moon in Virgo is born with a deprivation. He's often unable to digest—it's as though he is always hungry and lacks a strong constitution. He must usually deal with illness, all of which stems from the central nervous system, creating intestinal-tract difficulties as well as a tendency for allergies, asthma, or even arthritis (this is contingent on the rest of the chart). The Moon in Virgo is so prone to these afflictions that supplements of vitamins and minerals are highly recommended. Taking care of his health should be uppermost to Moon in Virgo.

Moon in Virgo is intellectual but feels put upon when he has to interact with others. This placement is not particularly conducive to being social and fun-loving. This is someone who works better behind the scenes.

MOON IN LIBRA

The Moon in Libra is a refined, gentle person who is charming and sympathetic. If afflicted, he can detach completely and give the impression of not being interested or involved when, in fact, he is dependent and feels almost incomplete without a partner.

Moon in Libra is always striving for peace and harmony, particularly in personal relationships, even if it means holding back or controlling emotions to avoid controversy.

MOON IN SCORPIO

Moon in Scorpio is a dominating and aggressive Moon. He tends to get moody and brood and is also terribly jealous. This jealousy leads to possessiveness and stubbornness. He is set in his ways—it's his way or no way—which makes for inequality and a somewhat archaic attitude, especially in a male toward a female. Moon in Scorpio females, having acquired the courage to display this quality, might dominate their home entirely too much, which is not conducive to a good relationship or equality in a household. It often leads to divorce.

Moon in Scorpio holds grudges and looks to get even. This brooder, who swings his emotions from one end of the pole to the other, requires self-control. However, when well-aspected, this is a powerful Moon. Under favorable circumstances, he can be successful, magnetic, strong, and self-reliant.

MOON IN SAGITTARIUS

In Sagittarius, the Moon combines with Jupiter. Jupiter expands, which makes Moon in Sagittarius yearn for freedom. He needs to be free to speak his mind and his truth. While he is friendly and can attract others with his gregariousness and optimistic attitude, don't count on the promises he makes because he's not going to keep them. Moon in Sagittarius is fickle. He makes a fine temporary companion, but in a serious relationship, he runs hot and cold. Should he be afflicted, Moon in Sagittarius might be a liar or overly extravagant.

Moon in Sagittarius is, by nature, a dabbler. Whatever is in mode, whatever is the style, he'll sniff it out but won't sink his teeth into it or do anything about it because he lacks the ability to get involved in anything that would lead to a commitment personally or philosophically.

MOON IN CAPRICORN

The emotions of Moon in Capricorn have a wet blanket over them because this is Moon/Saturn and Saturn is authority. Saturn restricts and limits emotional expression so it produces someone who takes himself seriously and is too stringent. This is a child with an old head on his shoulders. While he has strong ambitions, Moon in Capricorn is also looking for security and authority. On the inside, however, he is withdrawn, holding back emotions and coming across as undemonstrative and unsympathetic. If there are other influential and liberating aspects, Moon in Capricorn can be a serious and achievement-oriented individual.

Moon in Capricorn never forgets his beginnings, which are usually humble or restricted. Even if he becomes wealthy, he will always have feelings of deprivation and never take money or possessions for granted.

MOON IN AQUARIUS

Moon in Aquarius is ahead of his time and willing to move into new territories. Since he deals with everything from a mental/intellectual orientation, he does not deal with emotions—he tries to transcend emotions and winds up feeling nothing.

Moon in Aquarius is forgetful—he can't even remember events that were significant or traumatic to him. He doesn't want to remember. Because of this, he'll keep repeating the same patterns or mistakes over and over without learning his lesson.

If afflicted, Moon in Aquarius can be selfish, self-centered, and self-protecting. Or he might be a butterfly—friendly with everyone but unable to handle the intimacy of close relationships. Very likely, somewhere in his past, a bad or betrayed friendship left him scarred, and since he hasn't yet worked it out, he avoids the intimacy of friendship altogether.

MOON IN PISCES

The Moon in Pisces is extremely sensitive. It is not considered a particularly strong Moon, yet, oddly, it has the ability to survive. Whether it means having to drag a broken leg, overcoming obstacles, or dealing with emotional battering, Moon in Pisces has the grit to withstand anything and go on.

Nobody knows the depth of Moon in Pisces. He suffers a great deal and needs to separate from the world every so often to strengthen or energize. Should the rest of the chart be strong, Moon in Pisces can be one of the most sensitive visionaries—a dreamer who can carry those dreams to realization. Whatever he feels or senses can eventually be actualized. The Moon in Pisces is also multitalented, so, unless afflicted or lazy, he will most certainly achieve.

Moon Through the Houses

MOON IN THE FIRST HOUSE

When the Moon is placed within two degrees of the ascendant it is considered part of the ascendant. In this house, there will be too much vulnerability. The ego becomes entangled by emotions, and reactions are immature at best. It can lead to late maturation and physical endangerment.

MOON IN THE SECOND HOUSE

The handling of money and assets becomes unstable. The attitude swings from generosity to hoarding money for the sake of security.

MOON IN THE THIRD HOUSE

This Moon placement lacks the consistency needed for a good education. Concentration is easily disturbed, causing the loss of thinking power.

MOON IN THE FOURTH HOUSE

This Moon creates an emotional bond with Mother that doesn't allow for independence. The need to protect the self takes precedence over all other needs.

MOON IN THE FIFTH HOUSE

This placement produces strong emotions that need creative outlets. This individual can be a great host or cook or a great parent. On the downside, there is a tendency to seek personal pleasure or satisfaction that will sacrifice others.

MOON IN THE SIXTH HOUSE

In this placement, emotions will register on the body. Diet becomes important since digestion and assimilation will be disturbed. Those with this Moon position can work well in areas of medical care and service to others.

MOON IN THE SEVENTH HOUSE

This Moon shows an emotional need for a mate or partner. A person with this placement feels he can't function alone. He usually draws partners who are sensitive or moody.

MOON IN THE EIGHTH HOUSE

This Moon possesses a powerful sex drive that can replace love and affection. A beneficial quality is a psychic sensitivity toward the feelings or needs of others.

MOON IN THE NINTH HOUSE

The love of travel prevails, whether mentally, as in reading *National Geographic*, or physically, as in trips and explorations. This Moon will maintain and be faithful to the religion of his parents or acquire his own philosophy and hold fast to it.

MOON IN THE TENTH HOUSE

The Moon indicates what type of reputation will be achieved. Whether famous or infamous, this person will be before the public. The best direction for this placement is to make society's or the world's needs his concern.

MOON IN THE ELEVENTH HOUSE

Attracting friendships is not difficult, but sustaining and taking care of them is. Intimacy is uncomfortable. This Moon doesn't seem to know the difference between use and abuse. Fortunately, its superficiality will do little damage.

MOON IN THE TWELFTH HOUSE

The Moon releases the subconscious. The flow of knowledge is easy. Psychic abilities abound, making people with this placement either sensitive or withdrawn to solitude and isolation. The only way through this karma is to serve others without reservation. This also includes karma with Mother.

MERCURY

Mercury revolves around the Sun every eighty-eight days, which means that it goes full circle many times in a year. It is always in one of three positions: before your Sun Sign, in conjunction with (or on top of) your Sun Sign, or past your Sun Sign. It is never more than twenty-seven degrees from the Sun in any direction.

Mercury, which rules the signs of Gemini and Virgo, is the planet of communications. Two types of communication are going on at all times—that which you tell yourself and that which you tell others. You need to be careful of Mercury because, depending on its aspect, it can be the world's greatest liar, superficial to the point of distorting the truth.

Mercury talks to the Sun Sign, telling it what it thinks, whether right or wrong. It represents your mental activity.

Mercury Retrograde

A Mercury retrograde usually occurs every three months, so there are three or four Mercury retrograde periods per year, each lasting about twenty-one days. If you were born during a Mercury retrograde, it is a time to look inward. You will be inspired and moved to recognize your ideas and thought processes with clarity.

A person born when Mercury is in retrograde will have a communication problem. He can tell you what he thinks, but can't tell you what he feels. He doesn't connect well with his emotions because Mercury blocks them. There is also difficulty communicating with the self.

Mercury Through the Signs

MERCURY IN ARIES

Mercury in Aries means Mercury is quick. His mind is fast and enthusiastic. Mercury in Aries is flamboyant and child-like, and all those other things that are part and parcel to Aries. He tends to hit and run. He gathers information quickly but usually does nothing with it.

If afflicted, Mercury in Aries can have a bad temper. He is also somebody who likes to talk but who doesn't give the courtesy of listening. He cuts you off before you've finished your sentence, then starts talking about who knows what—not necessarily the subject at hand. Mercury in Aries needs to stabilize and learn control to become a better listener and impart more complete and relevant information to others.

MERCURY IN TAURUS

Mercury in Taurus produces a conservative mind that gives more leeway to others. He is often unsure about his thinking mechanism, so his mind operates in a slow, conservative manner. Don't underestimate it, however, because Mercury in Taurus possesses the ability to store and recall information. His methodical manner sometimes makes him insecure and feeling as if he's not up to date on information or as if he has been left behind. Maturity and experience release an artistic side of this Mercury.

MERCURY IN GEMINI

Mercury rules Gemini, so it is comfortable in this placement and knows what to do. It is a keen, alert, and restless mind that could become a think tank. The negative side of this is a tendency to overthink to the point of mental exhaustion. This intense thinking can lead to a confusion of the mind, the picking of other people's brains, and, consequently, jumping to conclusions. When afflicted, Mercury in Gemini lacks the consistency to gather facts or concepts. He cannot master a subject until he learns to stay focused. He must also learn to pace himself to avoid mental burnout.

MERCURY IN CANCER

Mercury in Cancer is a Mercury/Moon association. It is a good placement for absorbing information and for producing an excellent memory. Mercury in Cancer also has psychic healing ability—he can listen to, empathize with, and help others. This person would make a good psychologist or therapist or succeed in any career in the healing arts.

This is a sensitive Mercury—almost prickly. He has an underlying need to protect himself and his potent emotions. You cannot deal with a Mercury in Cancer from a rational point of view—he is going to resist and is not going to accept.

MERCURY IN LEO

Mercury in Leo doesn't trust easily. Since he thinks in an idealistic way, he interprets everything as some perversion of his idealism. He holds tough to his opinions and is not going to change—his mind is rigid and unwavering. Forty years from now, he'll still maintain the notions and attitudes he has today.

Mercury in Leo has faith only in that which is consistent. Whether that consistency leads to his falling behind or becoming out of sync with the rest of the world is something he doesn't seem to fathom or care about. He is going to do everything at his own pace and make progress slowly. He only trusts that which has been proven to him personally. When afflicted, his rigidity leads to extreme stubbornness.

MERCURY IN VIRGO

Mercury in Virgo is stable and staid. Because of that, this mind lends itself well to architects and engineers. This very logical mind takes on an earthlike quality and structure that can make for an exceptionally knowledgeable individual. However, it also makes for somebody who does not necessarily notice the impact of his words on others. He might be an excellent orator, but that doesn't mean that he will be interested in speaking on a one-to-one, selfless, emotional level.

Mercury in Virgo, with his analytical tendencies, looks for perfection in everything and everybody. When afflicted, he can be an intellectual snob who deems his mind better than anyone else's. No matter what your education, no matter what techniques you use to prove that you are comparable, he will look for and find some flaw—whether it be in the selection of your words or the fashion in which you acquire or pass on knowledge.

On the positive side, Mercury in Virgo can make an excellent teacher or accountant.

MERCURY IN LIBRA

Mercury plus Libra/Venus gives a finesse—a quality that can lead to speaking diplomatically but not necessarily with substance. He does not speak emphatically or passionately, nor reflect upon his feelings.

Mercury in Libra wants harmony. Ideally, he wants everyone to have a good time and be nice to one another.

If afflicted, he will speak in a militant fashion—almost making you feel like you ought to salute him—or be wishy-washy, noncommittal, and afraid to step on anyone's toes. Unless sustained by a group of stable planets, Mercury in Libra won't even remember what he told you. His communications are often detached and lacking in passion.

MERCURY IN SCORPIO

What a quick and powerful mind this is—it can reach the deepest recesses of the collective unconscious. The only problem with Mercury in Scorpio is that he expects others to be just as bright, quick, and knowledgeable. Scorpio is ruled by Pluto, and as such, he has power, directness, and freedom from inhibition. His mind works quickly and sharply in acquiring information, making him an excellent detective or diagnostician. Pluto is always underneath; it rules the underworld. And so, Mercury in Scorpio can get under things.

If afflicted, this is a difficult placement for Mercury. His mouth is going to open up and bury you. He will be harsh, cold-blooded, and unconcerned about any feelings you might have.

MERCURY IN SAGITTARIUS

Mercury in Sagittarius doesn't have the barriers that are necessary for concentration. So, while the mind is sharp and alert, it can't concentrate on any one subject to create a goal or objective. This mind goes here and there, touches this and that—but its impatience and inability to hone causes him to expound articulately about an ideal or philosophy without wholeheartedly believing it.

MERCURY IN CAPRICORN

Mercury in Capricorn is a sober thinker. He has a powerful ability to concentrate and an excellent memory. He is structured, detail-oriented, and great at remembering little anecdotes. But because of Saturn, he is not witty. Mercury in Capricorn tends to behave like a little old man since Saturn matures him way before his time or chronological age indicates.

Mercury likes security, so if afflicted, he will be fearful of the things he lacks. Mercury in Capricorn needs to become optimistic, which is challenging to accomplish because, by nature, he is incredibly pessimistic. He is always concerned with what he doesn't have rather than enjoying what he does have. Ironically, he can be an excellent achiever—that is, of course, if his pessimism doesn't get in the way and create psychosomatic illnesses or other neuroses.

MERCURY IN AQUARIUS

This is an excellent position for Mercury. Uranus is a subconscious planet and gives Aquarius an intuitive quality that borders on prophetic. The mind is sharp and resourceful. An affliction, however, can make Mercury in Aquarius opinionated because, since he sees further down the line and innately knows the outcome, he wants to bring it to the present. While he might be insightful and correct in his opinions and ideas, this prophetic quality can make him untimely in his judgment. If he is working alone, he can be ahead of the crowd and totally dependent on himself. Only when he's dealing with others do his stubbornness and convictions make him difficult to be around.

Mercury in Aquarius is a good position for a writer because it allows him to take his ideas and opinions and run with them successfully. If he becomes sensitive to group dynamics, he'll be timelier in his approach. If those around him are willing to accept his innovative, ahead-of-its-time thinking, Mercury in Aquarius can become productive in a group situation.

MERCURY IN PISCES

Mercury in Pisces has the potential to be a psychic visionary, one who is in touch with sensitive and artistic expression. Whenever Pisces appears, there is a multitude of talent, so expressions are made through many creative forms—writing, poetry, music, or dance.

Mercury in Pisces is not necessarily group-oriented. He feels, but cannot always cope, behaving in a moody, negative, and sensitive fashion. Mercury in Pisces picks up everyone else's moods and vibrations, which can be confusing because he can't always distinguish between what he thinks and feels versus what everybody else thinks and feels. So, depending on the atmosphere, environment, and circumstances, if he has a positive flow, he feels good and expressive. But if the conditions are unfavorable or emotionally difficult, he will brood and be moody and unstable. Mercury in Pisces should be careful to avoid projecting the negativity of his environment or else wind up becoming a victim of his surroundings. If this happens, he will become oversensitive and prickly. The best solution is to withdraw, regenerate, and then reenter that environment with complete self-awareness. Mercury in Pisces must learn to set boundaries and not worry about the what-ifs. If this is accomplished, he can become strong and productive.

Mercury Through the Houses

MERCURY IN THE FIRST HOUSE

This placement performs in a vital and alert manner. However, it also gives the individual the notion that what he thinks is more important than what others think. The thought process is emotionally based, creating nervous reactions.

MERCURY IN THE SECOND HOUSE

Mercury in this house produces speaking or writing ability. In fact, any kind of communication can be mastered.

This individual is business minded and an excellent moneymaker.

MERCURY IN THE THIRD HOUSE

This is a good student, curious and intelligent, who can excel as a researcher or investigator. He will have strong ties to his family. If afflicted, he will filter experiences through his intellect and avoid emotion.

MERCURY IN THE FOURTH HOUSE

High-strung thinking can cause high anxiety. The result of this placement is an unstable, erratic homelife, which can lead to isolation.

MERCURY IN THE FIFTH HOUSE

This creative mind can excel in writing and lecturing. Communications of all forms are fortified. Difficult aspects can cause an opinionated, fixed mentality.

MERCURY IN THE SIXTH HOUSE

Preoccupation with one's health can result from this placement. Worry, fear, or overwork will take its toll on the body. Proper nutrition, rest, and recreation can revive the central nervous system.

MERCURY IN THE SEVENTH HOUSE

Partnerships or marriage will become an intellectual experience instead of an emotional exchange. This person can spend too much time arguing and squabbling over incidentals.

MERCURY IN THE EIGHTH HOUSE

Communications must be clear. Lending or borrowing must be spelled out, and investments and contracts taken seriously—this will protect the inheritance of the person with this Mercury.

MERCURY IN THE NINTH HOUSE

Mercurial thinking needs stabilizing before this individual can acquire the religion or philosophy he longs for. Should he not settle down and avoid distractions, he will lose his objectives. In-laws could make his life a misery.

MERCURY IN THE TENTH HOUSE

Saturn extracts from Mercury a seriousness and a disciplined outlook. This individual will be aware that one's honor, reputation, or standing in this world is essential. He will attain the status he seeks unless an affliction prevents him from staying on a straight path.

MERCURY IN THE ELEVENTH HOUSE

Mercury, glib and light, can attract an intellectual entourage rather than friends. Friendships require emotional investment. To realize a goal takes thought and attention, but, unfortunately, this placement creates delays and interference with plans.

MERCURY IN THE TWELFTH HOUSE

Mercury can tap areas of the individual's psyche that he can't share with others. Information will be available to this individual from a source he can't understand. If there is no affliction, he may make use of it; otherwise, he will become afraid of it.

VENUS

Venus revolves around the Sun every 225 days. Venus rules the signs of Taurus and Libra and is associated with passive and feminine qualities. In a male, the passive quality of Venus is displayed as harmony and devotion—the ability to cooperate with others.

Venus in a chart produces "class." It is associated with refinement and beauty on all levels.

Venus says, "I want." Venus is there to produce self-love, which, kept in balance, is an important quality. On the negative side, however, it can be self-indulgent and self-serving.

Venus Retrograde

If you were born during a Venus retrograde, your inability to appreciate the self is apparent. You are unable to express self-love. You don't know how to get what you want or how to satisfy the self. You must learn not to expect such things from others but, instead, develop them within yourself.

Venus Through the Signs

VENUS IN ARIES

Venus in Aries has a challenge—it's a clashing situation where Venus is going to be worn out by Aries's mode of "action without thinking." Venus in Aries is headed in one direction—the fulfillment of a central desire or ego—and so, he becomes impulsive. There's a tendency to fall in love with love rather than fall in love with the person, making Venus in Aries shallow, inconsiderate, and untrustworthy. One day, he can be charming and flirtatious and the next day stomp all over everything until it is torn apart. With one hand he builds, and with the other he destroys.

VENUS IN TAURUS

Venus rules Taurus, so it's quite at home here. In Taurus, Venus possesses a powerful, earthy quality. Its physical, sensual, and emotional responses are emphasized. This is a Venus that wants to stroke and be stroked. An individual with this placement is the comfort-acquiring / comfort-giving type who won't be sloppy, unconcerned, or jealous. Unless afflicted, Venus in Taurus will not be competitive nor want to upstage anyone—he recognizes his worth and is comfortable and happy with himself and what he brings to others.

VENUS IN GEMINI

Venus in Gemini is charming and witty but somewhat superficial. Emotions are lacking depth. The mercurial quality of

Gemini produces inconsistency and disinterest in experiencing emotions. His charm attracts many people, and he gets along well with his family, but don't try to pin him down. Like a butterfly, he cannot be harnessed. He will entertain you and please you but will eventually leave you. An affliction to this placement can create a compulsive talker who wants understanding from others but is unable to reciprocate.

VENUS IN CANCER

Venus in Cancer, unfortunately, has a changeable, moody, "today he wants this and tomorrow he doesn't want it" inconsistency. The pleasure response of Venus in Cancer comes more from an emotional than an intellectual base. He is always looking for security. That security might be education, self-sufficiency, or dependence on a mate. Because of the Moon's influence, this person tends to do a lot of mothering or smothering. Instead of being her partner's equal, a woman with Venus in Cancer plays a "you need me" role, which can prove detrimental to her relationships. In the male, Venus in Cancer can be committed to his family and partner because his feminine side is empathetic and sympathetic to whatever is necessary to maintain a home and family. If Venus in Cancer is heavily afflicted, he will always feel that he cannot get what he wants and will wind up feeling empty or deprived.

VENUS IN LEO

When Venus is in Leo, you can actually see the drama—that colorful character is projected through Venus. Everything is a passion. Venus in Leo doesn't just like something, he loves it; he doesn't dislike something, he loathes it. Nothing and nobody in this world can change a Venus in Leo into anything other than what he is, so you might as well leave him alone and accept him.

Venus in Leo is a lover of good things—good wine, good food, good surroundings, good people. If afflicted, he might overindulge himself and be taken in by flattery. He tends to be attractive—Venusian qualities are really emphasized by the influence and vitality of Leo's ruler, the Sun, so this person is, basically, a star. He is going to be methodical but also have a flair. Leo has a majestic quality that shines through Venus, all of which are very attractive, all of which attract. Venus in Leo likes attracting—he loves an entourage, loves the admiration of others. Even if afflicted, this dramatic Venus in Leo will not suffer or get into trouble—his dignity doesn't seem to fail him. He is thoroughly refined.

VENUS IN VIRGO

Whenever a man has Venus in Virgo, he is looking for the perfect woman. He winds up having trouble relating to women because he's analyzing instead of simply loving. He breaks his relationships apart to see what love is made of. Sadly, by the time he discovers what love is made of, he's lost it.

In a woman, Venus in Virgo is the proverbial nun—none today and none tomorrow. She is good at serving, maintaining a household, and is quite fastidious, but this is not someone who will hug you. She is not demonstrative or approachable. You'll only hear from a Venus in Virgo when something is wrong. If everything is okay and acceptable, there are no praises. But if there is a problem or flaw—and she will definitely find one—the criticism will begin.

A woman with Venus in Virgo is not likely to attract—she's not charming and doesn't have the feminine softness that is so attractive in Libra or Taurus. She comes across as a difficult person to deal with and will have trouble finding and keeping a mate. Venus doesn't do well placed in Virgo—not for the male or the female.

VENUS IN LIBRA

Venus is comfortable in Libra. He is airy and free to take flight of fantasy. He is intellectual and loves everything artistic and refined. Venus in Libra can bring some beautiful qualities or refinement to a person. His emotions are under control, and he doesn't hold a grudge.

If afflicted, however, it is just the reverse—this is somebody who is not going to trust you. If you hurt him once, you'll hurt him again, so he winds up holding a grudge.

Venus in Libra makes a wonderful host. He loves to create an atmosphere of total comfort and beauty. However, if there is any upheaval or discord, or if anything gets out of whack, Venus in Libra's physical well-being, particularly the nervous system, will be affected. Nevertheless, both men and women with Venus in Libra look for the tranquility and the joy of everything beautiful, and do not want grossness or disruption around them.

VENUS IN SCORPIO

Venus in Scorpio is concerned with all that is physical and carnal. Naturally, Venus resents this because Venus is basically the love principle. He wants tranquility, refinement, and love. Because of Scorpio's water quality, Venus in Scorpio is going to appear sedate and softer than he really is. He will act as if everything is under control when, in fact, he is actually suppressing. A militancy is hidden within this individual because, underneath, Scorpio is active and forward moving—he presents himself with great force. He wants others to know exactly what he wants, regardless of whether it might be inopportune or incorrect. He lacks all inhibition and can be rude and crude.

Venus in Scorpio is a detrimental placement because these two planets, Venus and Mars, are in conflict. If afflicted, sexuality takes over. Instead of being "in love," Venus in Scorpio falls "in lust" without understanding the difference between the two.

VENUS IN SAGITTARIUS

Venus in Sagittarius links Venus with Jupiter, the two aspects that are associated with love. This individual is open, affectionate, and kind to others. Venus in Sagittarius has a theoretical mind and wholeheartedly believes that everybody should love one another. While he is caring and loving, he cannot necessarily sustain a relationship for the long haul—displaying affection and falling in love are two very different things to him.

If there is an affliction to Venus in Sagittarius, he becomes a hard gambler, obsessed with the idea and thrill of taking risks.

VENUS IN CAPRICORN

Venus, combined with Capricorn's ruler, Saturn, can create a rather strange love nature. Venus in Capricorn feels that he must take himself seriously and proceed with caution in all ways. As an earth sign, the ego sensitivity often associated with Capricorn makes him act with caution in the pursuit of love. Therefore, Venus in Capricorn matures into a passionate and love-oriented individual. In his youth, he is somewhat restrained and withholding, even afraid. Until he overcomes the fear that keeps him aloof, he will use that restraint as a shield or mask to prevent him from succumbing to love.

If afflicted, this will become the kind of restraint that doesn't allow Venus in Capricorn to trust another person, feel love, or even feel as if he is genuinely loved by others. Sadly, this is difficult for those close to him to alter. Love is to be felt, and if you don't feel worthy of love, no matter how much someone loves you, it won't make a difference. Venus in Capricorn must learn that he is, in fact, lovable and must be open to love for his loving qualities to mature, blossom, and be satisfying.

VENUS IN AQUARIUS

In Aquarius, Venus is not only detached but calm and downright cool. Venus in Aquarius finds it difficult to understand his emotions, his ability to love, and to demonstrate love. He is not always understanding of or comfortable dealing with the emotions of others. He intellectualizes love, which is an empty and ultimately lonely circumstance. As such, Venus in Aquarius must learn one important thing—to become a friend. Once Venus in Aquarius acquires friendship or friendliness toward others, he can eventually move on to a loving situation.

Venus in Aquarius often develops the ability to love and understand later in life. If not, his relationships and marriage will be unfulfilling and suffer. When detached, Venus in Aquarius functions strictly for the self, which prevents good and enduring interactions with others.

VENUS IN PISCES

What a delight. Venus, which is love, combines with Neptune, which is the deepest of all the constellations. This creates a unique type of love—a willingness to sacrifice, a lack of fear, and a deep-rooted passion. There is, with Venus in Pisces, the ability to touch the soul.

Venus in Pisces is poetic, a lover of art and music, and extremely psychic. Venus in Pisces can't be fooled—he knows when he's loved, and he also knows when he is not loved. A male with Venus in Pisces has a gentle and feminine side. This is a man who has refinement, who can appreciate a passionate opera or a tear-jerking film without feeling as if his masculinity is threatened.

Venus in Pisces can go beyond the call of duty. If afflicted, this romantic nature, this ability to romanticize everything, is going to backfire. When confronted with the flaws and limitations of other people, Venus in Pisces becomes disappointed and disillusioned. When love rules a situation and things go awry, it brings great unhappiness. This is a hurdle that Venus in Pisces must overcome—he must take off the rose-colored glasses and see the world for what it is.

Venus in Pisces believes everyone deserves love, but needs to recognize that self-love is of equal importance. He must learn to appreciate the self, foster one-to-one relationships, and reimagine his view of universal love.

Venus Through the Houses

VENUS IN THE FIRST HOUSE

Venus will project into this placement an attractive but vain personality. The world will respond cooperatively. Should it be afflicted, this native will be lazy and unconcerned.

VENUS IN THE SECOND HOUSE

This placement brings a keen eye for what is beautiful, which can lead to profitable investments. It will attract all measure of financial wealth or help. Bad aspects to this house can produce excessive spending.

VENUS IN THE THIRD HOUSE

Venus here has a soothing effect on the mind and makes for a pleasant disposition. An interest in music encourages artistic and creative abilities. Aspects will determine if this easygoing manner will turn into laziness.

VENUS IN THE FOURTH HOUSE

This person loves to be home. He will share, entertain, and can handle all aspects of social/political gatherings. If not afflicted, there will be a good relationship with Mother.

VENUS IN THE FIFTH HOUSE

Love is not wanting for this placement. This is an attractive and charismatic personality to which the opposite sex will respond. There is also an ease with children, whether as a parent or with youngsters at large. An affliction can lead to overspeculation.

VENUS IN THE SIXTH HOUSE

There will be a peaceful atmosphere at work or at home. Venus will excel in any career that requires diplomacy. Should there be an affliction to this house, illnesses can occur caused by excess or some loss of balance. Moderation is the key.

VENUS IN THE SEVENTH HOUSE

Marriages and other legal partnerships will be favored. The love that is attracted by Venus in this house makes for long marriages. If afflicted, there might be more than one marriage but no lack of love.

VENUS IN THE EIGHTH HOUSE

Legacies will be protected, whether they be from a partner or other family members. Inheritances, including those incurred in a past life, are covered. An affliction can create a preoccupation with sex.

VENUS IN THE NINTH HOUSE

The pleasure afforded to this native has no boundaries. This is a traveler who can indulge in and appreciate foreign cultures. This individual also actually loves his in-laws. An expansion of consciousness enables one to relate to all philosophies. Should there be an affliction, prejudice takes over and a bad attitude prevails.

VENUS IN THE TENTH HOUSE

The world loves you! If you love the world, it will reward you with all measure of success. In business, it will open doors—the reputation alone will be a passport. If afflicted, scandal occurs, which will result in a fall from high office.

VENUS IN THE ELEVENTH HOUSE

The support and cooperation from friends benefit the objectives of this native. The proper use of organizations can lead to a satisfying life. Negative aspects to this house can create a people abuser who will only be self-serving.

VENUS IN THE TWELFTH HOUSE

How do you get what you want? This placement doesn't make it easy. Venus in this position must be clear and direct about its desires or be left behind. If high-minded, the native will seek a spiritual life doing "God's work" on Earth. This is an excellent placement for meditation. If afflicted, the individual will isolate and escape through alcohol or drugs.

MARS

Mars revolves around the Sun in 687 days, coming to its original point in a chart once every two years. Mars rules Aries (and before the discovery of Pluto, it ruled Scorpio) and is associated with temperament.

When Mars makes contact with the Sun, it develops an energy that enables you to take action. Mars, well-aspected, can move mountains. Negatively aspected, it can be one of the biggest destroyers because it fosters action without thought.

Mars is associated with the initiation of relationships— love affairs, marriages, business partnerships, and so on. Relationships often appear to go through two-year cycles that relate to the orbit of Mars. Whenever Mars comes back to its original position, which is called a *Mars return*, it frequently creates upheaval in relationships. This upheaval isn't necessarily negative; it is an opportunity to review and assess existing circumstances or, in the worst case, eliminate them.

Careers are also influenced by Mars since the planet is

almost always associated with a job—the end of one or the beginning of another.

Mars is a generator. When Mars is cycling, it gets people up and rolling. Since Mars rules muscular structure, it creates an energy that spurs movement. When Mars is in conjunction with any planet, it energizes it.

Mars Retrograde

During a Mars retrograde, the ability to act is curtailed. It is as though you have been victimized by others simply because you are not using your aggressive qualities correctly—you either don't know how to be aggressive or you fear aggression. You water down your energies. This does not make for a happy person; it creates someone who internalizes his aggression and anger. This is dangerous because a retrograde Mars can lead to brooding or nursing old wounds and, eventually, to health problems ranging from ulcers to anxiety. Anger that cannot be externalized winds up being internalized, which impacts one's health. Retrograde Mars in a chart indicates the inability to displace its natural energy positively or productively.

Mars Through the Signs

MARS IN ARIES

Mars in Aries has energy and physical/mental capabilities. He's quick. He's a little firecracker who moves with enthusiasm.

Mars in Aries afflicted is going to be bad-tempered and an unstable personality who acts before he thinks. Of course, his intentions are good—he has good ideas—but because he doesn't stop to think, he's bound to get himself into trouble.

When a male demonstrates this type of behavior, it is usually acceptable, but females with this placement are challenged—they develop an aggressive stance that is often viewed as problematic by the outside world. If a female with Mars in Aries begins to experience difficulties, developing a little self-discipline will go a long way.

MARS IN TAURUS

Taurus is ruled by Venus, which has a slow and deliberate quality. So, when Mars comes along and shakes it up, it creates a personal push/pull situation. Mars activates Venus in a peculiar way. Instead of being self-loving, it makes him self-centered, giving the individual no other objective than self-gratification. Mars in Taurus will find himself overindulging—in food, drink, sex, and so on.

As a youngster, Mars in Taurus is not allowed to express these self-indulgent qualities, so he winds up being outwardly cool and sedate, while inside, his suppressed qualities are churning. Mars in Taurus is slow to burn, but once he explodes, he's also slow to cool.

If afflicted, that resentment is multiplied; the selfishness becomes central, and the need to protect the self becomes overwhelming, prompting him to lash out at anyone who threatens him. An afflicted Mars in Taurus can be dangerous—he's a little spark ready to ignite and can be-come a great, big fire if the rest of the chart doesn't mitigate or displace this afflicted quality. Self-discipline is necessary and important for Mars in Taurus to master. With self-discipline, he can take this energy and channel it into a productive activity like sports. Otherwise, his temperament will be his downfall.

MARS IN GEMINI

Mars in Gemini is contradictory. He is able to act at two levels—he can be intellectual, witty, chatty, and friendly, but if his innate emotional insecurity kicks in, he can sud-denly turn nasty. Mars in Gemini has a quick tongue, and that doesn't necessarily mean keen or alert; it means that he speaks through both sides of his mouth. In essence, he's a pretty good liar. The natural Gemini duality of intellect versus emotion becomes activated and exaggerated by Mars, making it difficult for him to reconcile the two. He wants to be in both places at once, which is impossible and frustrating.

Should Mars in Gemini be afflicted, it will create a ner-vousness that could result in stuttering or the inability to complete sentences. The mind is going to wear down the body, producing nervous ticks and other psychosomatic ill-nesses.

MARS IN CANCER

Can you imagine every single emotion that a human be-ing possesses, fired up? That is Mars in Cancer. Talk about extremes—this individual is so emotional, sensitive, and prickly that he's going to wind up full of fear and insecurity. He will, more than likely, spend his life feeling as if somebody kicked him in the stomach. This is a challenging placement for Mars, even when the rest of the chart is well-aspected. If there is an affliction, Mars in Cancer will be prone to stomach disorders, bleeding ulcers, or too much in the breadbasket. Mars in Cancer must control and displace his emotions rather than swallow them. If kept in the gut, it is a sure bet that those emotions will burn a hole right through the stomach or accelerate all the digestive juices, making Mars in Cancer hungry all the time. This will result in obesity and many other unpleasant side effects in addition to moodiness and bad feelings.

MARS IN LEO

When Mars joins the Sun, there is no end to the energy—it is overwhelming. Mars in Leo is going to leave everybody else in his dust. He's a born leader who wants to make absolutely sure that he is heard and understood. He wants to be the leader of the pack.

If afflicted, he can become indignant. He is going to challenge authority and be hard to hold down. He'll also wind up getting into lots of trouble. Because he pushes his will, as most fire signs do, no matter how wrong he is, Mars in Leo will insist he is right. He will become quarrelsome and annoying—not the type of person others want to deal with. Mars in Leo will roar. He will become bombastic and melodramatic, feeling as if he hurts more than anybody else. He will start to overdo it, and his vitality will prove troublesome for him.

Leo rules the heart, so Mars, which produces a bad temper when afflicted, can lead to heart problems. Mars in Leo must learn to cool off and chill out.

MARS IN VIRGO

Mars in Virgo is a tireless worker who loves the labor but has an endless obsession with details. He possesses an energy that, when well structured, is productive and successful. If he comes from the viewpoint of analysis instead of criticism, he will react to things positively instead of becoming angry and quarrelsome. Afflictions can produce a critical, demanding, and unfeeling personality. The results, unfortunately, are loneliness and a feeling of rejection that the native doesn't understand. On the other hand, when well-aspected, Mars in Virgo has a self-regulating attitude that can lead to cooperation and productivity.

MARS IN LIBRA

Mars in Libra is easygoing, lazy, and not too self-reliant. Though Libra is a militant Sun Sign, with the influence of Mars, he becomes more dependent, although he still intends to dominate. The scales of Mars in Libra can tip from one side to the other. One day, he can appear smooth and diplomatic, acting with a great deal of finesse, and at other times, he'll turn into the pushiest, nastiest, "get out of my way" person with an attitude that can be ice-cold.

Mars in Libra makes many plans but can't seem to get them off the drawing board. He sits and vacillates, wondering if he needs somebody else to help get his plans in order. When afflicted, this is a militant general—demanding, unconcerned, and lacking compassion.

MARS IN SCORPIO

Mars in Scorpio has intense emotions, which are projected without inhibition. This is an overbearing personality that needs to be tempered. He must learn that it is much better to attract with honey and softness than through sheer force. He needs to learn to draw from love rather than fear.

Mars in Scorpio can instill fear in others and intimidate—he's a real bully. Mars in Scorpio needs to recognize that bullying does not come from strength but from weakness or insecurity. While he can be powerful in whatever he undertakes, his pushiness can prove a real turnoff to others.

MARS IN SAGITTARIUS

Something inside Mars in Sagittarius makes him feel he can take chances yet land on his feet. He has an inner knowing. Although it might appear to others as impulsiveness, it is actually behavior that is very directed. It has a source and an intuition that become apparent even before Mars in Sagittarius has taken that action.

Should there be an affliction . . . watch out! He cannot be held down to anything. He's unreliable, and the chances he takes are not inspired; they are just plain old gambles. Mars in Sagittarius sees every challenge in life as a gamble. His ultimate desire is to bring the will of the universe into his control—Sagittarius is perhaps the most willful of all the fire signs. Hence, when afflicted, with Mars energizing, it creates a "get out of my way, here I come" attitude. Mars in Sagittarius is so open and up-front that you know way before he arrives that he is coming and you're going to have to contend with him. He's going to be blunt and tactless. He can be self-righteous and needs to recognize the rights of others.

MARS IN CAPRICORN

This is probably the best Mars placement in the Zodiac, especially if the rest of the chart indicates ambition. Mars in Capricorn is disciplined and capable. As an adult, he thrives. However, as a youngster, he is restricted by Saturn (Capricorn's ruler) and behaves almost like an old person, taking on more responsibility than the average child should bear. That situation really takes the fun out of being a kid. But as Mars in Capricorn matures, a rather strange reversal takes place—Saturn releases him and he becomes self-reliant. He can slowly and methodically reach the top of the mountain. The only way he will fall off is if he hasn't been ethical.

This strong and capable Mars in Capricorn, if afflicted, becomes someone who is a little slow on the uptake. While organized and productive, with an affliction, pessimism will set in, producing an inability to use his acquired knowledge. He will be closeted and double-check himself all the time, which eventually becomes his undoing. He can be quarrelsome, challenge authority, and take on a "think what you like" mentality.

MARS IN AQUARIUS

Mars in Aquarius pairs Mars with Uranus, a strange combination that can lead to trouble. Mars in Aquarius is more than likely going to be out of step with family, peers, business colleagues, and partners.

Mars in Aquarius has an innate desire for freedom and a relentless need to know. This often makes him quarrelsome—he just doesn't let up. When dealing with a Mars in Aquarius who becomes argumentative, don't pick up the issue. Drop it, let it go, and turn your back because he will just continue to argue and force his so-called concepts and ideas upon you.

Mars in Aquarius can be untimely. If he isn't brought under control, he could well be speaking the truth but at the wrong time. He'll blurt out his thoughts and opinions and take over without considering someone else's need to express himself. Mars in Aquarius is capable of bringing down the establishment.

MARS IN PISCES

Mars in Pisces is a control freak. Its Neptune rulership produces fears. Mars can exaggerate those fears and bring about a personality that is aggressive and domineering, someone who will try to jump over people's heads, acting purely out of fear. Pisces carries subconscious fears or memories from past lives.

The quest for Mars in Pisces is to conquer and overcome his fears. Once that is accomplished, Mars in Pisces becomes calm. Calmness is necessary because it restores vitality. This is important because, if afflicted, the innate fears and aggressions of Mars in Pisces can create illness.

Mars Through the Houses

MARS IN THE FIRST HOUSE

The personality is intense, quick, and brash. There is a physical strength and energy that must be displaced carefully; otherwise, the person will find himself in dangerous positions. Self-confidence can turn into egocentricity if afflicted. A bad temper will be his undoing.

MARS IN THE SECOND HOUSE

The resources of this house can be energized, leading to the accumulation of assets. A good education or plain hard work will make for gains. Mars is volatile, and an affliction can lead to the loss of all that has been gained.

MARS IN THE THIRD HOUSE

The mental faculties must be kept positive in this placement. Negative thoughts can cause nervous tension and irritability.

The quickness of mind can lead to quarrels with everyone around him. The mental energies can best be displaced by study and higher education.

MARS IN THE FOURTH HOUSE
Mother's attitude is reflected when Mars sits in this house. We live what we are taught, so constant discipline over emotions is necessary to avoid chaos. An affliction can create difficulties from birth until death.

MARS IN THE FIFTH HOUSE
The energy of Mars propels this person to seek and reach the limelight. He will display unusual strength and fortitude in the pursuit of his goals. Should this house be afflicted, disappointment and sorrow will surround the children of this native.

MARS IN THE SIXTH HOUSE
This individual should take care not to become a workaholic. To achieve successful relations with coworkers, this person needs space and some degree of solitude. If afflicted, he will revert to a cold, intellectual attitude that will be troublesome.

MARS IN THE SEVENTH HOUSE
Mars doesn't allow partnerships or marriages to succeed. The individual tends to be bad-tempered. He feels "his way

or no way" is the only solution. If afflicted, the battle will inevitably lead him to divorce court.

MARS IN THE EIGHTH HOUSE

War will rage over money or legacies. Sexual attitudes or activities will dominate the personality. If afflicted, he will find himself embroiled in the misuse of occult knowledge.

MARS IN THE NINTH HOUSE

This person is off to see the world and to dabble in foreign cultures. He will probably research religion or philosophy. Poorly aspected, this placement can turn one into a fanatic.

MARS IN THE TENTH HOUSE

This Mars placement can carry a business or military man to heights of prestige. Discord with Dad can make for a runaway. This pattern will cause friction with all authority. A negative attitude will place his reputation at risk.

MARS IN THE ELEVENTH HOUSE

Be careful of whom you call "friend." The need to be sociable can lead to dangerous associations. The lack of integrity for personal advancement can be the undoing of this placement.

MARS IN THE TWELFTH HOUSE

This Mars appears diluted. A person with this placement doesn't always know how to displace his energy. Nevertheless, if harnessed, this quality can be creative in handling hidden enemies or any other threat. An affliction can lead to explosions of suppressed hostilities.

JUPITER

Jupiter takes approximately twelve years to revolve around the Sun. Jupiter is a lucky planet that can provide realization. Jupiter allows you to relate to others and to yourself. It taps into emotions and increases the ability to empathize. Learning to distinguish between what you think and what you feel results in self-awareness.

Jupiter, which rules Sagittarius, expands. It triggers human physical development. It influences the menstrual cycle in females and the onset of puberty in males, both of which usually occur at the age of twelve, precisely the number of years it takes Jupiter to make a complete revolution around the Sun. It spends one year in each house.

Jupiter rules the liver, which is the seat of anger. When negatively impacted, it can create physical or hormonal difficulties within an individual.

Jupiter Retrograde

A retrograde Jupiter usually leads to an overbearing individual, especially if placed in the fourth house—it is a tyrant in that house. It creates an inability to empathize with others, which results in an insensitive and isolated individual.

Jupiter Through the Signs

JUPITER IN ARIES

Jupiter in Aries produces an appropriate sense of self and strong self-esteem. He possesses a quick mind and a great deal of strength and energy. When equipped with solid skills and education, Jupiter in Aries has leadership skills and makes a good executive. He's a bit of a risk-taker, too. Whether it is a risk in business, the stock market, or taking a risk himself, with his "I can do that" attitude, he will take chances with the highest sense of optimism.

If afflicted, this risk-taking tendency might turn to gambling or lead him to live in the fast lane. By and large, however, Jupiter in Aries does well.

JUPITER IN TAURUS

Love is in the air! Jupiter in Taurus is the ultimate lover of everything. He is fond of luxury, fond of culture and elegance, and fond of an upscale, material-filled environment. He is immersed in sensuality. He has a hearty appetite for food and sex. Jupiter in Taurus is bent on looking for all the comforts and joys of life.

You can't push a Jupiter in Taurus—he will stubbornly stick to his guns even more. He's quite content enjoying and smelling the roses and anything else that comes his way. The price he pays comes in later years when those overindulgences turn to overweight.

JUPITER IN GEMINI

Jupiter in Gemini takes his emotion and intellectualizes it so that he winds up not caring. He doesn't want to expend emotion. He'd rather filter it through his head, which doesn't work. This individual tends to be self-centered, which imposes a natural separation and isolation from everyone else. He does not attract friends or wealth.

Jupiter doesn't do well in Gemini. He scatters his energies and avoids listening to his heart. When his forked tongue surfaces, he loses credibility.

JUPITER IN CANCER

Jupiter in Cancer really cares. He has a nurturing and caring instinct that makes for a compassionate and attractive personality. His manner says to others, "I want to take care of you. I want to benefit you." This is one of the most selfless Jupiters of the Zodiac.

A woman with Jupiter in Cancer is a loyal and loving mate because she is the proverbial mama who will make chicken soup and take care of her home, husband, and children. A man with Jupiter in Cancer is a good provider. He is artistic and senses what others need. He also works well with the public.

Jupiter in Cancer should watch those calories because this placement can lead to weight problems, usually caused by a lack of digestive enzymes.

If afflicted, Jupiter in Cancer is one of the tightest wads going—a crab that battens down all the hatches and goes down under. An afflicted Jupiter in Cancer has an enormous fear of starvation, so he gets overly bossy and wants to rule—the children, the spouse, the dog, the cat—and hangs on to every cent he can get his hands on.

JUPITER IN LEO

Jupiter in Leo is an excellent and vital placement since Jupiter combines with the power of the Sun. In fact, all through the Zodiac, whenever Jupiter conjuncts the Sun, regardless of the constellation, it means you have a guardian angel. That's because the ability to contact the self, that flow between the conscious and subconscious, is very pronounced in this position.

Jupiter in Leo possesses self-reliance, courage, and loyalty. This individual is magnanimous. He is a true leader and a capable executive. If afflicted, he can be victimized by his pride and desire to impress others so that he is likely to fall prey to anybody who can stroke his ego, usually for their own advantage.

JUPITER IN VIRGO

Expansive Jupiter tries hard to operate in what is probably one of the more insecure signs of the Zodiac. Virgo is practical, intellectual, and critical, which can restrain Jupiter. Instead of expanding and becoming optimistic, the opposite occurs, and pessimism sets in. If afflicted, Jupiter in Virgo relates to others not only from an intellectually critical point of view but also from a condemning point of view. He is always looking for the dirty spot. This afflicted quality condemns others so that he can feel better because he suffers from inner condemnation. Jupiter in Virgo, in this stance, is never going to be content nor find anything worthwhile. He is nitpicky, critical, irritable, petty—paying too much attention to little nothings and making him impossible to deal with. About the only place such characteristics have value is in the field of investigation. Other than that, Jupiter in Virgo must learn to stop picking away at the little things. He needs to get past the details and look at the much bigger picture.

JUPITER IN LIBRA

Jupiter in Libra is friendly and outgoing. A lover of beauty, he can be successful in the arts. Jupiter in Libra is also going to be attracted to the law—Libra is the constellation of law, so lawyers and judges often have Libra in this placement (or in other planets in their charts).

An affliction can prove troublesome since Jupiter in Libra might not hold up his end of a partnership. This can lead to problems in a marriage or business relationship. He will be focused on self-interest and sensual pleasures rather than the everyday consistency necessary to succeed in any profession, business, or personal relationship.

JUPITER IN SCORPIO

Scorpio can be subtle, covert, and secretive—it is his nature. Jupiter in Scorpio relates to others in a conservative manner, keeping to himself and keeping things close to his vest. This is a person you will usually find in police work. He could also probably excel in engineering or medicine. In the right line of work, he is both practical and successful. Jupiter in Scorpio is analytical and an excellent diagnostician. He can even regenerate himself from illness or the mistakes of poor decisions.

If afflicted, his secretiveness becomes almost devious; he might know what can help you but keep it to himself and avoid getting involved. With this kind of affliction, Jupiter in Scorpio must learn how to care for other people in a loving, positive way and not out of self-interest.

JUPITER IN SAGITTARIUS

Jupiter rules Sagittarius, so it is in domicile position here. It creates one of the most optimistic, freewheeling, outgoing, and happy individuals around. He enjoys everything, especially those things that take him outdoors—nature, horses, sports, and so on.

Jupiter in Sagittarius is a natural financier. He has an uncanny ability to attract money. If he makes a two-dollar bet, he wins big; if he drops a quarter into a slot machine, dozens pour out of it. This financial success is not gender-specific—a woman with Jupiter in Sagittarius can successfully compete with men because she possesses excellent executive qualities.

Jupiter in Sagittarius has a unique, almost metaphysical aspect—the ability to bend the will of the universe. If he says he's going to do it, miraculously, through his positive thinking, he will make it happen.

Unfortunately, if afflicted, Jupiter in Sagittarius is going to go haywire. This is a gambler—he's going to make a million and lose a million. His great love of horses will lead to gambling, or his great love of traveling and the outdoors will lead to wanderlust. His love of freedom might make him irresponsible and lead him astray.

JUPITER IN CAPRICORN

Capricorn's ruler is Saturn, and Saturn and Jupiter contradict each other—when one says, "Go," the other says, "Stop." This puts Jupiter in Capricorn in a bad situation. He's just going to plod along. He'll get ahead in the world, but he's going to be overly cautious and pessimistic throughout the journey.

Jupiter is optimistic and Saturn is pessimistic, which gives Jupiter in Capricorn an internal push/pull. This meticulous and careful individual, who is penny-wise and pound foolish, is always afraid of losing, so he's certainly not going to take a chance.

As Jupiter in Capricorn matures and learns that no one is out to get him, he can loosen up. He can even make some money if he invests it rather than hanging on to it.

If afflicted, unfortunately, loosening up will be the very thing he can't do. Jupiter in Capricorn afflicted means that this person will spend the rest of his life hanging on to everything for fear that he will lose. There's only one bottom line for Jupiter in Capricorn—to stop worrying about losing and start taking chances.

JUPITER IN AQUARIUS

Jupiter in Aquarius is interested in science and groundbreaking projects; he is a reformer. He's the consummate humanist bent on changing the world, ending hunger and poverty—fighting the dragon at every corner.

Jupiter in Aquarius is forward-thinking. He's extremely original, yet being ahead of his time sometimes makes for an unconventional individual who might or might not succeed. For example, Albert Einstein had Jupiter in Aquarius, and look how far ahead he was—he was exploring concepts and formulas that took years to be accepted.

When afflicted, Jupiter in Aquarius always has his foot in his mouth. Instead of being that organizer, that world leader, that person ahead of his time, he is just going to be discontented, always taking things apart for examination. He will be thinking in terms of what you should be doing, what you ought to be doing—he is very theoretical, but, unfortunately, that doesn't mean he knows what is good for you or for himself.

JUPITER IN PISCES

Jupiter in Pisces can relate to others emotionally. He is quiet and interested in nurturing and caring. He has an innate sense of how the other guy feels, how not to step on his toes, and how to encourage him to be the best he can be. That doesn't necessarily mean that Jupiter in Pisces can encourage himself. He doesn't seem to have self-ambition or self-betterment and is not looking for it either. He believes that if he does good for others, somehow or another, good will automatically come to him.

With his exceptional ability to empathize, Jupiter in Pisces is comfortable and successful in any humanistic setting—at the hospital, at a shelter, at a hospice. He thrives tending to children, whether in childcare or helping youngsters who are ill or troubled. Jupiter in Pisces can transcend all the limitations that most people have, allowing his rare talents to benefit others.

Afflicted, Jupiter in Pisces has a tremendous fear of pushing the self. He will be a very retiring individual, perhaps even lazy. At times he will need to stand up and be counted, and Jupiter in Pisces is afraid of just that.

Jupiter Through the Houses

JUPITER IN THE FIRST HOUSE

Jupiter is associated with expansion, so the ego can create an optimistic individual or a self-indulgent personality. The good fortune of this placement is often seen as a "guardian angel." If there is an affliction, his weight will get out of control.

JUPITER IN THE SECOND HOUSE

This position gives financial prowess. The individual can deal with others' finances and assets while securing an impressive portfolio for himself. However, should an affliction to this house exist, the losses can be significant.

JUPITER IN THE THIRD HOUSE

Feel good about yourself! The family will cooperate and responses will be positive. This native can be a good student, usually one who needs a great deal of mental stimulation. With an affliction, there will be restlessness and loss of concentration.

JUPITER IN THE FOURTH HOUSE

Good family relationships are displayed in the fourth house. The native will be aware of his soul and create a peaceful and content environment. He will know good fortune until the end.

JUPITER IN THE FIFTH HOUSE

Lucky you! The expression of creativity in all forms is yours. Children will be a blessing, and you will know how to enjoy all good fortune. On the other hand, an affliction will force a payback for any neglect in past lives.

JUPITER IN THE SIXTH HOUSE

In this placement, health and the work environment are a pleasure. Hard work and dependability will be rewarded. If there is an affliction, health will suffer. Jupiter rules the liver, so temperament and diet can stress that organ and create illness.

JUPITER IN THE SEVENTH HOUSE

What a great catch! Partnerships or marriage will benefit from all aspects. Plenty of love, money, and social position guaranteed.

JUPITER IN THE EIGHTH HOUSE

A great deal of emotional or sexual energy is released here, coupled with the ability to regenerate oneself. Legacies are also covered. If afflicted, poor judgment will lead to extravagances that can be costly.

JUPITER IN THE NINTH HOUSE

Here is the world traveler who is always on the go and off to foreign shores. He will succeed, whether philosophizing, writing, or teaching. Afflictions will interfere with the juggling of his personal and professional lives.

JUPITER IN THE TENTH HOUSE

What a climber. Right to the top of the ladder of success, he attracts opportunity and cooperation from others. His place before the public will be assured unless there is an affliction, in which case he will fall from high office in disgrace.

JUPITER IN THE ELEVENTH HOUSE

Choose your friends wisely. The promise of a vibrant social life and help from friends will occur as long as an affliction doesn't produce poor judgment. If afflicted, there will be a downfall of objectives and a life of strife.

JUPITER IN THE TWELFTH HOUSE

The lesson here is that being right is not enough—one must also be timely. This placement allows the native to tap the reservoir where all past-life experiences await. With good judgment, this individual can apply lessons learned to meet the challenges of his life. Hidden enemies will fall by the wayside since a guardian angel is at work. Success can be achieved in the medical field, investigative work, or research. An affliction can produce a person who is quick to judge—not necessarily wrong, just untimely. The native should learn to hold his counsel.

SATURN

Saturn revolves around the Sun approximately every twenty-nine and a half years. Saturn is a somber and restrictive planet. It deals with the responsibilities you take on and work through. The ancients feared Saturn because it was a warning of limitations.

Saturn is the first of the karmic planets, meaning it relates to unfinished business, usually from a past life. Wherever Saturn is placed, it demands that something be accomplished. If you haven't taken care of your responsibilities, Saturn is not going to let you proceed. Saturn is a restrictor; it will confine. It can restrict you in numerous ways, from a broken body to the limitations of your finances.

With Saturn, there is a lesson to learn and a lesson to

teach. Through Saturn, we grow and develop, both physically and mentally. It is the planet of maturation. Saturn makes absolutely sure that you will reap what you sow. Saturn has been referred to as the "old man of the sky." It will not let you get away with anything that is not part and parcel of your positive development or evolution.

Saturn rules Capricorn, the midheaven, and the tenth house.

Saturn Retrograde

Saturn retrograde relates to self-worth. The inability to judge oneself accurately shows up in a retrograde Saturn. Saturn, as a maturation planet, puts your self-worth into proper perspective. People who tend to place more importance on themselves than on others will undoubtedly learn the lesson—Saturn will restrict them until they balance their own worth with the worth of others.

Saturn Through the Signs

SATURN IN ARIES

Saturn is restrictive, and Aries, with its Martian energy, just wants to run amok. So, Saturn in Aries is going to be one frustrated individual. Early in life, this child will probably get into trouble—run and then hit the wall. As a result, he begins to develop suspicion and becomes distrustful and holds back, whereas, ordinarily, Aries runs and jumps without thinking. Saturn in Aries holds an innate fear that the authorities over him—parents, teachers, clergy—are somehow going to stop him. The fear might even produce guilt, which will make him feel he is doing something wrong and stop him in his tracks.

The problem with Aries, in general, is that he starts but never finishes; but in this placement, Saturn will hold him down and make him finish. As he matures, with Saturn stabilizing the energy of Mars, Saturn in Aries will make slow, productive movement. He will be more successful in his middle to older years. He has mental power, is exceptionally bright and intelligent, and is always adventurous.

Should Saturn in Aries be afflicted, he will simply hold back and repress. He will suffer from headaches, and his whole body will begin to stagnate. His natural thinking, physical prowess, and fiery, dynamic personality will be dampened.

SATURN IN TAURUS

Saturn in Taurus will learn a vital lesson in the value, cost, and price we pay. Whether it be an emotional price, a physical price, or a material price is incidental. He needs to understand that what he has acquired and what has been given to him is in no way detrimental—that he should not deny himself his honest due.

If Saturn in Taurus gets involved with excesses, he will immediately pay. He needs to learn that material needs are not essential—his self-worth is not determined by the material but within himself.

If afflicted, Saturn in Taurus is going to learn some hard

lessons. There is extremism in Saturn in Taurus that must be brought into balance. It's either complete denial or complete indulgence, neither of which is acceptable or healthy. Saturn in Taurus is afraid that if he doesn't glut himself, he will starve, or if he doesn't amass possessions, he will wind up destitute. It will take a great deal of strength for Saturn in Taurus to come to terms with these extremes and take things in moderation.

SATURN IN GEMINI

Gemini is an intelligent constellation, so when Saturn is in Gemini, it controls that butterfly "hit-and-run" quality that makes Gemini superficial. Instead, Saturn in Gemini is disciplined. He begins to think and does some deep soul-searching about himself and about life. His adaptable nature teaches him how to strike the right balance between his intellect and emotions. With Saturn in Gemini, he stabilizes, and his mood swings are not quite as high or as deep.

If Saturn in Gemini is afflicted, instead of stabilizing, he will swing back and forth like a pendulum. He will wind up having either a lot of central nervous disorders or dermatological problems.

SATURN IN CANCER

The Saturn in Cancer personality is based on fear. He is frightened and pessimistic and, as a result, hell-bent on protecting himself. Early in life, he looks for his parents to protect him and begins to feel sorry for himself, which creates a selfishness that is always in need of justification. Often, his fears become self-fulfilling prophecies—Saturn in Cancer sometimes feels so darn sorry for himself that nobody wants to be around him. He'll get closed up and involved with the self, which only leads to loneliness and the inability to share, trust, or attract others.

In this loneliness, Saturn in Cancer can become ambitious and shrewd, but he will rarely be generous. If afflicted, he'll just lock himself behind the door, draw the curtains, and not bother with anybody because he's afraid that nobody wants to deal with him. By this time, it's important for Saturn in Cancer to learn how to get out of himself and reach out to others.

SATURN IN LEO

Saturn in Leo might find it difficult to believe that somebody truly loves him for himself, and so he walks around puffing out his chest and telling everyone how wonderful he is because he doesn't really believe it.

Saturn in Leo not only gets pompous but strong-willed—he's going to have things his way for fear that he won't get his way at all. It's that old "hit before you get hit" situation. Saturn in Leo carries a chip on his shoulder that doesn't let up.

If afflicted, Saturn in Leo is going to get in trouble with

the law. He'll be the kid who gets into trouble in school. He's going to be pushy, demand attention, act up or act out—doing all the disruptive things kids do to get attention. Saturn in Leo needs a lot of positive stroking to reassure him that he is, in fact, important. The healthiest thing Saturn in Leo can do is calm down and give to others the love and respect he wants, because, ultimately, he will get back what he gives. Humility must be learned.

SATURN IN VIRGO

Saturn in Virgo has an orderly, analytical mind that can find or break down all the details, making a good accountant, bookkeeper, researcher, or scientist. Saturn in Virgo feels productive and capable when working alone. He often has difficulty with coworkers because he is so detail-oriented that those around him who are not will prove exasperating to him.

Saturn in Virgo has to avoid becoming an intellectual snob. Everyone holds a talent in a different place so that, collectively, we become great. Saturn in Virgo must learn that he only plays a certain part within the group.

When afflicted, Saturn in Virgo tends to panic. He nags and nitpicks and can wind up wreaking havoc with his central nervous system. He gets flaky, hits the wall, and becomes accusatory and hysterical until things fall into place. Saturn in Virgo has difficulty dealing with the stimulation of other people's thoughts and ideas, desires and needs. That is why he works better alone.

SATURN IN LIBRA

Saturn in Libra takes seriously all those qualities that Libra represents—equilibrium, partnership, cooperation. This individual understands the balance between his ego and another person's ego. Saturn in Libra develops the type of patience, understanding, and cooperation that appreciates and allows others to explore, explain, do—he doesn't need to jump on their heads or upstage them. Saturn in Libra innately knows what it takes to keep the wheels rolling so that everybody can move forward.

If afflicted, where partnerships are usually successful, they become just the opposite. Instead of cooperating, Saturn in Libra detaches and becomes lazy, afraid, and dependent. This leads to difficulty in all types of relationships, especially in marriage.

SATURN IN SCORPIO

Saturn in Scorpio has a great deal of inner strength, but it requires a great deal of careful handling. He has a healthy ego and sense of self-importance. He is a shrewd individual with a strong lust for power who needs to learn discipline and self-control.

If afflicted, Saturn in Scorpio is extremely jealous, possessive, and vindictive. He can love passionately or hate bitterly. He'll imagine that somebody is doing something personally to him—he interprets everything as a personal affront.

If not brought under control, Saturn in Scorpio can overpower the influence of the Sun. This is a problematic aspect that can either positively empower a weak chart or create danger in a strong chart. When afflicted, Saturn in Scorpio can turn into a self-seeking, power-hungry individual who will find himself in great emotional and physical pain as a result of his drives. He needs to watch his gallbladder, which is particularly vulnerable.

Being resourceful, Saturn in Scorpio is out to get what he wants, even if he destroys himself and others. If he can become self-disciplined, it will prevent him from falling prey to his own destructive tendencies.

SATURN IN SAGITTARIUS

Saturn in Sagittarius has a quest for the truth. He looks to understand. He is naturally philosophical, regardless of his religious or philosophical background. An innate quality within Saturn in Sagittarius allows him to be accepting of circumstances and in the know. Because of that, he is outspoken—there is not a fear within him. Even when challenged, he will just shrug and remain unfazed. He possesses a well-honed intuition that empowers him with assuredness.

Saturn in Sagittarius is a superb communicator who can take on any mental challenge set before him. His mind is keen, flexible, intelligent, and able to hold its own among peers.

An affliction makes Saturn in Sagittarius careless and indifferent. That seeker of the truth becomes plain old argumentative and wants to challenge for the sake of challenging, which overshadows his respectable mind. You have to turn your back on him because he'll just babble to make a point. He will home in on what he thinks is your weakest point and attack you right there, even though it might be out of left field. He'll bring in the kitchen sink to win an argument. He'll know where to hurt you and how to deviate from an argument to win, believing that he who shouts the loudest wins.

SATURN IN CAPRICORN

Saturn rules Capricorn, so it is very much at home here. This individual knows what power is in its purest form. It gives him prestige and a strong sense of responsibility toward his family, the neighborhood, or business. He selflessly gives way to the support and concern of others. As Saturn in Capricorn matures, he acquires humility and masters one of his greatest fears—the fear of deprivation.

If afflicted, this goal of power and mastery will take over, and Saturn in Capricorn becomes hell-bent on squashing or putting his thumb on other people. He becomes extraordinarily selfish and will wind up alone, brooding, since nobody will want to deal with him. Saturn in Capricorn can also manifest physical conditions that affect the joints, bones, and entire skeletal structure.

SATURN IN AQUARIUS

Saturn says, "Stay"; Uranus says, "Go." So, Saturn in Aquarius starts out early in life insecure about who he is and what he is about. He always finds himself having to do for others.

For the first half of his life, Saturn in Aquarius lives with a continuous and challenging quest for identity. He is forever wondering, "Where do I belong?" Whether it be within the community or country, or an identity with his heritage, he needs to find the answers and integrate them into his personality. He must take responsibility for himself.

Fortunately, as he approaches midlife, he usually discovers who and what he is about. Once Saturn in Aquarius establishes this, he comes to peace at last.

On the other hand, if there is an affliction, there will be a great deal of anxiety. The circulatory system comes under pressure, making Saturn in Aquarius uptight and depressed. He will need to go inside himself to establish his sense of belonging.

SATURN IN PISCES

Saturn is a restrictor, so that means Saturn in Pisces restricts himself. Everything becomes emotionally charged. It is often a negative charge since he becomes fearful, clinging to the past, worrying and carrying it around on his shoulders, convinced that if something happened before, it will happen again. As a result, Saturn in Pisces is not daring. He is going to tell himself repeatedly, "I can't win," and, most certainly, he's not going to win—his fears will become self-fulfilling prophecies. Saturn in Pisces must learn to overcome this anxiety; otherwise, he'll wind up carrying the world on his shoulders.

If afflicted, Saturn in Pisces needs the compassion of others because he must work hard and diligently to come out of his shell, face the world, face his ghosts, and let go. He must learn to let go of the past.

Saturn Through the Houses

SATURN IN THE FIRST HOUSE

This placement makes for an old personality who will be responsible for everyone. He is seeking approval because he doesn't feel loved. Shy and unassertive, he needs to overcome the feeling that he is not important. If afflicted, selfishness and self-importance will take over and make for an intolerable person.

SATURN IN THE SECOND HOUSE

The poor man's mentality must be modified. The quest for real estate or hard work without end doesn't make for peace of mind. Saturn can attract inheritances, but one's attitude will determine the value.

SATURN IN THE THIRD HOUSE

Education must be taken seriously and will require consistency and overcoming interruptions and delays. Family life can be a responsibility that weighs heavily. Depression lurks in this placement, which has a serious and deep mentality.

SATURN IN THE FOURTH HOUSE

The fear of separation from family can lead to unhappiness. Clinging to the past will prevent the independence needed to grow and develop. The stomach will be particularly vulnerable.

SATURN IN THE FIFTH HOUSE

The responsibility for children is prevalent in this placement. Their care and needs will take priority. This could also be the aspect that doesn't allow for reproduction. In this event, the native can resolve this limitation by working as a teacher or in any field that serves children.

SATURN IN THE SIXTH HOUSE

Rewards come only to those who work hard for them. The lack of recognition could push this individual into demanding irrational feats from himself, sacrificing his health in the process. Developing a healthy attitude toward the environment will pay off well.

SATURN IN THE SEVENTH HOUSE

This placement makes for a loner—someone who can do it all by himself but who must also learn to cooperate. He is sensitive and shy but doesn't want anyone to know. He will probably marry for security.

SATURN IN THE EIGHTH HOUSE

The demand in this sector is of restraint, whether it be sex or any other appetite. Striving for balance in all things can regenerate this placement. Financial difficulties are inherited through a marital or business partner.

SATURN IN THE NINTH HOUSE

The continuation of a past-life philosophy or religion takes hold early in life. The individual holds on to his beliefs throughout life and evolves to a higher level. Saturn can, if afflicted, go out of balance and produce a fanatical religious zealot.

SATURN IN THE TENTH HOUSE

Dad might not be there to create an example or image. This placement needs to guard against misusing power or a fall is guaranteed. Ambitious and self-reliant, he will climb the ladder of success, but he can't afford to forget service or payback to others.

SATURN IN THE ELEVENTH HOUSE

Discipline is the path necessary to achieve all the goals and objectives of this native. Rewards or achievements will arrive, but only in due time. If patient and honest, hard work will produce a satisfying mature life. Should the wrong types of association become important, all plans can go awry.

SATURN IN THE TWELFTH HOUSE

Like any other planet placed in the twelfth house, the source of past-life qualities can be tapped. Each emotion faced at the conscious level produces a liberation of the personality. It allows for the dissolution of attitudes produced by negativity. In turn, the native comes forth and reaches out to others.

URANUS

Uranus takes eighty-four years to revolve around the Sun, spending seven years in each house.

Uranus, which rules Aquarius, is slow-moving and slow to impact. What you see in Uranus is usually the tip of the iceberg because it is a subliminal planet, a planet of the subconscious. Uranus deals with your individuality and your personal identity—not as others have told you that you are but who you discover you are. Uranus makes you unique and unconventional.

Uranus Retrograde

For those born with a retrograde Uranus, the action of Uranus, which is slow, becomes even slower. The unique and unconventional quality of Uranus ceases to be because something is undeveloped that must be cultivated to emerge and grow. This creates the late bloomer, one who doesn't readily discover his rare individuality.

Uranus Through the Signs

URANUS IN ARIES

Uranus plus Aries's rulership of Mars is a difficult combination. These two planets will do the unexpected. Uranus in Aries is ready to jump and to pioneer. He possesses a spirit of curiosity that motivates him. He is a real trailblazer.

If poorly aspected, Uranus in Aries is rebellious. He can really undo himself or trip himself up. The results can be the loss of a job or physical endangerment. Uranus in Aries has an innate suspicion and fear—the worst fear is of being rejected.

URANUS IN TAURUS

Uranus in Taurus plods along slowly and meticulously. He holds on to all material possessions that he feels can be refurbished or salvaged. Uranus in Taurus has a difficult time because Uranus is looking to bring in the new and get rid of the old, while Taurus feels as though everything is being pulled out from under him and changing too quickly. Since Taurus is a fixed sign, he likes to take his time. He needs to think and plan and will do wonderful things in his own way and time. When pushed, however, he can never be sure whether he did the right thing.

When afflicted, Uranus in Taurus has difficulties in love affairs—the refined influence of Venus, the ruling planet of Taurus, has no influence, causing partnerships to deteriorate. He will make demands on his partner, many of which are unrealistic. In this placement, negatively afflicted, the innate harmony of Venus will turn to discord. Vulgarity will emerge, and force, rather than love, will motivate his actions.

URANUS IN GEMINI

Gemini is an air sign that is looking to balance. Gemini wants to be intellectual, use the mind, and communicate.

Uranus speeds this up. It makes the mental faculties sharp and quick, so ideas flow. People with Uranus in Gemini succeed in anything having to do with communications (such as radio and television) or with conveying ideas and concepts (as in teaching or writing).

If afflicted, Uranus in Gemini will create difficulties with others, especially relatives. His restlessness will make him tactless.

URANUS IN CANCER

Uranus in Cancer is insecure and often feels sorry for himself. He feels he isn't cared for or loved enough, so he becomes prickly, touchy, and erratic, feeling that too many demands are placed on him. The underground function of Uranus stirs emotions from a subconscious level. It also makes for a problematic homelife, especially in the early years.

Cancer represents home, so Uranus in Cancer is bent on improving the quality of his homelife.

URANUS IN LEO

Uranus in Leo is forthright and self-aware. He believes he has control over his destiny. He is bold and adventurous. Should he be high-minded, his intelligence and courage will entice him to accept challenges.

If afflicted, Uranus in Leo is a petty tyrant. He will be vain and destructive and trample on and use people for his own well-being.

URANUS IN VIRGO

Uranus in Virgo has an analytical mind that seeks the truth. He is a reformer and an activist. A civic-minded person, he advocates safety, healthy living, a clean environment, and the like. This person is conscious of what indiscriminate living can produce.

If afflicted, Uranus in Virgo will become a hypochondriac and excessive worrier.

URANUS IN LIBRA

Uranus in Libra deals with the law. The symbol of Libra, the scales, represents justice. The law has a spirit that is often overlooked, so Uranus in Libra will revisit the law.

People born with Uranus in Libra are interested in love, beauty, and harmony, but not in the traditional sense. These people explore the arts. They will look for independence in marriage that is not traditional.

If afflicted, individuals with this placement should be wary of kidney ailments.

URANUS IN SCORPIO

This is a solid and favorable placement for Uranus. It produces a powerful individual, someone who possesses a strong will and the persistence to forge ahead despite confrontation.

Uranus in Scorpio can thrive in the medical field as a surgeon, healer, psychologist—any area that involves probing, digging deep, looking for causes and cures, or trying to get to the bottom of all the ills of the world.

Uranus in Scorpio is very black or white. He can be an angel or a demon. His energy must find an outlet for better or worse. With Uranus in Scorpio, all emotions surface. If afflicted, this individual can be susceptible to drug abuse or trafficking, cults, and the like.

URANUS IN SAGITTARIUS

Uranus in Sagittarius creates audacity and rebelliousness—especially toward that which is orthodox and conventional. Uranus in Sagittarius supplies the need to expand one's personal horizons and to research and understand various philosophies for evaluation and application.

Sagittarius rules the thighs and hips, so, unfortunately, if afflicted, Uranus in Sagittarius will have to contend with lower-back problems, especially the sciatic nerve.

URANUS IN CAPRICORN

When well-aspected, Uranus in Capricorn can take a stuffed shirt and turn him into a lighthearted individual who's willing to take a gamble—Capricorn normally never gambles or takes chances. Uranus in Capricorn might undertake politics or some other prestigious undertaking that will allow his need for authority to blossom. If afflicted, he's going to put on cement boots and be as rigid as can be. And rigidity causes the body to suffer—the skeletal system and the digestive system.

Uranus in Capricorn constantly deals with the push/pull of "Should I, or shouldn't I?" He will have to resolve the home-versus-profession issue. The resolution is this: When he's home, he's wonderful and faithful; when he's out of town, there's no accounting for what he's going to do. The best solution for Uranus in Capricorn is to let go, enjoy, and not be afraid.

URANUS IN AQUARIUS

In Aquarius, Uranus is in domicile position. He is intellectually far ahead and scientific-minded. This is the New Age in mentality—to get rid of the old to make way for the new. The problem with this attitude is that Uranus in Aquarius needs to develop compassion and understanding to overcome his detached, impersonal manner. This attitude works fine when dealing with a group, but it becomes problematic in a one-on-one situation. If afflicted, it makes Uranus in Aquarius downright cruel. He has an indiscriminating mouth that might be correct but, nevertheless, spits in your face.

Uranus in Aquarius must learn to develop some compassion and soften up because he can be a hard person. The way to reach this person is through logic and reason, or to just develop a thick skin.

URANUS IN PISCES

Uranus in Pisces, because of its Neptune rulership, is an uplifting combination. Neptune is a planet with no form;

Pisces deals with old fears and sorrows, and the what-ifs. Uranus in Pisces puts a halt to all that and begins to break up the old patterns. Neptune is an inspiring planet but has a way of slipping through your fingers because it can't be harnessed. But when Uranus is in Pisces, it fences in Neptune and gives it a form. As a result, Neptune begins to reinforce the intuition of Pisces, giving it enormous comprehension, psychic ability, understanding, and sensitivity. Because of its sensitivity, Uranus in Pisces needs isolation. It must get away from the crowds and overstimulation to relax and recharge its nervous system. When afflicted, the native often escapes through drugs, alcohol, or sex.

Uranus Through the Houses

URANUS IN THE FIRST HOUSE
The ego will undergo changes. It will appear to be erratic and impulsive. The native doesn't know what he wants or how to go about getting what he wants. Uranus will isolate him until he learns how to be cooperative.

URANUS IN THE SECOND HOUSE
There will be feast or famine depending on the rest of the chart. This person must be willing to invent innovative methods of earning his income. This is not a good placement for someone who wants a fixed or predictable income.

URANUS IN THE THIRD HOUSE

The native will feel somewhat isolated and different from the rest of the family, particularly brothers and sisters. If he becomes extremely unconventional, he will suffer. Education will be interrupted unless interest and willingness are maintained.

URANUS IN THE FOURTH HOUSE

Mother may not be dependable, causing emotional difficulties for the native. The homelife will repeatedly be upset, whether through moving from place to place or because the family undergoes financial changes.

URANUS IN THE FIFTH HOUSE

Unconventionality displays itself in this house. The children of the native might prove exceptional or, if there is little discipline, terribly destructive. Cooperation is of utmost importance or romance will not survive. Creativity is high but can be of an unusual nature.

URANUS IN THE SIXTH HOUSE

An ingenious personality, but this native will need an environment where he can move about. Boredom can lead to psychosomatic illnesses. The central nervous system is vulnerable. Self-control will be his best medicine.

URANUS IN THE SEVENTH HOUSE

Partners of this native will be difficult and uncooperative, demanding great discipline from the native. Divorce or separation will most likely be the outcome. Maturity can produce a successful but unconventional union.

URANUS IN THE EIGHTH HOUSE

This placement calls for caution. Uranus and Mars together are always dangerous. Bad tempers can create havoc, whether it be with partners or on one's health. Sexual habits will need control. Money, especially inheritances or partners' wealth, can disappear unexpectedly.

URANUS IN THE NINTH HOUSE

The philosophy or religious background of this native may not be orthodox, leading him through various experiences. He will probably deal with foreign affairs, which will, in turn, supply him with teaching or publishing successes.

URANUS IN THE TENTH HOUSE

Uranus's placement here is an indicator of the student of astrology. It can produce an original and humanistic occultist. This placement carries a karma that can only be displaced, not altered.

URANUS IN THE ELEVENTH HOUSE

This placement can produce a person who deals with all measures of people. He could be the social worker who deals with troubled people or the serious businessman who succeeds through the management of others. This native will most likely "find himself" late in life, as his goals and objectives are in constant flux.

URANUS IN THE TWELFTH HOUSE

The twelfth house can be a place of confinement or liberation. The fashion in which the native handles one or the other will surface from the reservoir of past lives and foster growth. It can allow a multitude of talents to reveal a new and prosperous path.

NEPTUNE

Neptune, the ruler of Pisces, is the other planet of the subconscious. It takes 165 years to revolve around the Sun, spending fourteen years in each house.

The glyph of Neptune is a three-pronged fork. One side of the fork is illusion and the other side is delusion. The middle prong, which is crossed, takes that illusion/delusion aspect, puts it on the cross of matter, and tests it. This is symbolic of how Neptune operates.

Neptune is elusive and difficult to harness. Neptune is like sand slipping through your fingers. People who have Neptune transiting through certain sectors of their chart are kept from flowering, achieving, and acquiring—that is the reason they are late bloomers. When Neptune moves on, these individuals can finally take back control of their lives and be constructive, even if this occurs in later years. There is no deadline as to when one can start over and produce something worthwhile.

Neptune can inspire you to pursue unbelievable and creative things; it is an endless source of information and talent. But Neptune must be conquered—otherwise, it produces nothing but fear, which will hold you back.

Neptune is vast and deep. It rules the ocean, fog, and oil. It deals with subliminal things, below the level of consciousness, so that many people do not realize until after the fact that Neptune has undone them.

A dangerous planet, Neptune is associated with drug and alcohol abuse. It is not a planet to be messed with. Even when you are handling Neptune, you can never be sure that it is under control. It is challenging to bring to form and to conquer.

Neptune Retrograde

Neptune in retrograde is a humdinger. Neptune is a difficult planet, so in retrograde action, the negativity of Neptune becomes prominent. Neptune has a depth that can be lifesaving, but when it turns retrograde, it goes underground and doesn't surface. All the wonderful concepts, ideas, and creative forces that are generally in Neptune when it is well-aspected will produce irrational fears and anxieties when in retrograde position. These fears are considered irrational because they are usually not created within the context of this lifetime but from past-life issues and unfinished business.

If born with a Neptune retrograde, it is necessary to maintain faith and courage in the face of all challenges.

Neptune Through the Signs

NEPTUNE IN ARIES

Neptune in Aries seeks alternatives and brings new perspectives to spirituality and the meaning of life. Here, the imagination is sparked, which can bring about changes in art and music. This energy can be impulsive, so people with this placement often think and react with passion but without concern for consequences.

NEPTUNE IN TAURUS

Neptune in Taurus focuses on material possessions and sensual indulgences. These needs are a double-edged sword. Although there can be great appreciation for and involvement in art, fashion, music, and beauty, there is also the tendency toward hedonism and overindulgence in possessions, food, drugs, alcohol, and sexual partnerships, which can have detrimental effects both personally and financially.

NEPTUNE IN GEMINI

Neptune in Gemini expands the mind, explores concepts and ideas, and brings about the fulfillment of hopes and ideals. The mind is restless in this placement, looking for development, innovation, and intellectual pursuits.

NEPTUNE IN CANCER

Neptune in Cancer is nostalgic. People with this placement tend to cling to their ancestral heritages because identity, home (and homeland), and family ties are important. If lacking compassion, karmic lessons are experienced.

NEPTUNE IN LEO

This is not a good placement. Neptune clouds judgment, making it unable to see facts and truths with clarity. As a generation, those with Neptune in Leo were reared during World War I and could not clearly see what was happening politically in Europe during that era. They were, ultimately, fooled by those infamous, rising dictators.

People born with Neptune in Leo, if afflicted, have trouble giving, receiving, or understanding love.

NEPTUNE IN VIRGO

Neptune in Virgo produces tension, fears, and stress. The term *psychosomatic* was coined during this transit, and nervous tension, particularly stress, was observed as a cause of many illnesses.

On the positive side, this transit drives people to serve their fellow man and the world. It can create the true humanitarian.

If afflicted, Neptune in Virgo can be self-centered and self-serving, critical, and always looking for flaws.

NEPTUNE IN LIBRA

Neptune in Libra looks for partnerships and alliances. On the negative side, those with this placement can be prone to divorce.

Historically, more wars occurred during this transit than in others. However, sustaining harmony and love, which is native to Libra, can end conflict.

People with Neptune in Libra have strong artistic tendencies and will develop new and creative art forms.

NEPTUNE IN SCORPIO

Neptune in Scorpio highlights escapism. Negatively influenced, it can mean escapism through alcohol, sex, and drugs. Positively influenced, it can bring self-awareness through meditation and psychic study.

Many with this placement will contend with the results of their parents' actions, which they will overcome through a sense of discipline their parents didn't have.

NEPTUNE IN SAGITTARIUS

Neptune in Sagittarius brings truth. It is a strong position. Sagittarius has a cognitive ability and an innate knowing that makes it seem lucky. Here is where the seed of truth surfaces. It provides an opportunity to decipher, clean up, and rectify. It is a time to look at old or orthodox concepts and see if they're still applicable.

Natives with this placement are open-minded and

idealistic, even when the world around them presents challenges or disappoints. Those with Neptune in Sagittarius must go beyond their personal boundaries, physically and economically. If afflicted, the native will lack judgment and be indecisive.

NEPTUNE IN CAPRICORN

Neptune in Capricorn brings clarity of thought to the individual. People with this placement are often innovative and ambitious and make strides in business and finance. They are goal- and detail-oriented, and approach things thoughtfully and methodically.

NEPTUNE IN AQUARIUS

Neptune in Aquarius represents evolution. It can carry on, rectify, turn around, and, most importantly, evolve. Many have revolutionary ideas, particularly in areas of communication and technology, often as a means of personal connection. They are inspired to improve the world through innovation and humanitarian endeavors.

NEPTUNE IN PISCES

Neptune in Pisces brings spiritual growth, idealism, and compassion. Natives with this placement are motivated to serve others, foster peace, and protect their environment. Many possess an innate sensitivity that will make them intuitive or demonstrate psychic abilities.

Neptune Through the Houses

NEPTUNE IN THE FIRST HOUSE

In this placement, the ego suffers, and the lack of reality surrounding this native is emotionally difficult. He must control and alter attitudes to feel comfortable with his interactions. Although he might know what he wants, he doesn't know if he deserves it. Few people will really know him.

NEPTUNE IN THE SECOND HOUSE

This placement is not going to allow you to keep your resources to yourself. The inability to clearly see how others manipulate or help themselves to your assets will produce losses. The beauty of this aspect is that if you choose to share, there will always be a refill. The flow is not interrupted.

NEPTUNE IN THE THIRD HOUSE

This placement can create an artistic imagination if supported by the rest of the chart. A lack of clarity can create a poor student, so there is the need to harness the mind and concentrate. Karmic lessons may make family relationships, particularly those with brothers and sisters, a challenge.

NEPTUNE IN THE FOURTH HOUSE

Home and family conditions will never be smooth or settled. The native will find himself being sacrificed or surprised by circumstances he can't control. Alcohol or other neurotic afflictions will bring unhappiness until the native moves away from the source.

NEPTUNE IN THE FIFTH HOUSE

This is an excellent placement for an actor because personal dramas can be played out through many roles. The inability to find a love can lead to affairs or dead-end relationships. There will be great sacrifices yet few rewards. Until they reach adulthood, children can prove to be a burden.

NEPTUNE IN THE SIXTH HOUSE

This person must be his own doctor and resort to natural forms of healing. Diagnoses are almost impossible—although the symptoms are evident, the causes are hidden. The sensitivity of this native creates a vulnerability that can prevent him from functioning with others. Isolation is not the best option, yet it is often what saves the native.

NEPTUNE IN THE SEVENTH HOUSE

The romantic aura that surrounds any partnership undertaken can cloud the dependencies or imperfections of the union. Sacrifice, the keynote of Neptune, produces fantasies and dreams of the perfect marriage. Even if he gives his power away, the native remains stronger and more capable than his partner.

NEPTUNE IN THE EIGHTH HOUSE

Neptune disperses all that would be gained either through a partner or a legacy. This native must not use his strength for his own gain because he owes others. He will be the keeper of others' souls. He could be an excellent financier if he serves the public.

NEPTUNE IN THE NINTH HOUSE

The mind of this individual becomes clouded, rendering him unable to articulate. His thoughts might be high-minded or mystical but not tangible. This person might give the impression that he lacks sympathy because he will indulge in intellectual, theoretical concepts while missing the emotional contact.

NEPTUNE IN THE TENTH HOUSE

This Saturn house extracts a karmic lesson. The native will never receive credit for work done unless he has earned it. Authority in this person's life will have proved irresponsible. He must take the mature role and overcome his obstacles.

NEPTUNE IN THE ELEVENTH HOUSE

All dreams and hopes can be fulfilled if they are defined and supported. This native must be careful of whom he calls a friend. He must understand human nature to avoid the deception that surrounds him. Others will want to ride his coattails.

NEPTUNE IN THE TWELFTH HOUSE

Since Neptune rules the twelfth house, we would think all is well. Not true. This placement can be the cause of irrational fears. A feeling of isolation can stress the native until he is ill. Finding a connection to a deity or fellow man can keep this native from suffering.

PLUTO

Pluto is a small, dense dwarf planet situated in the outermost position among all the planets.

Pluto, which was discovered as a planet in 1930, was reclassified as a dwarf planet in 2006 because it did not meet the criteria newly established by the International Astronomical Union (IAU). In astrology, however, Pluto is still considered influential due to its powerful and transformational qualities. Its discovery ushered in extraordinary world changes and precipitated the Great Depression in the United States and the rise of Nazism in Europe.

Pluto takes 248 years to revolve around the Sun, but its course is erratic. Since its discovery, it has increased in velocity, spending less and less time in each sign, and now lasting approximately fourteen to thirty-five years. It has speed, carries information, and can awake, shake, and bring things to the surface. Pluto rules earthquakes; it rules anything that is subterranean, whether at the physical, emotional, or mental level.

Wherever Pluto is in your chart, it makes enormous demands. It will present the greatest challenges of your life. Since Pluto moves quickly through each constellation, it produces rapid changes, generational changes. Although there is no permanency with Pluto, it never winds up taking away what you need.

The regenerative powers of Pluto are endless and can impart enormous strength to human beings. Pluto is authentic, but it requires mastery. It will not let you get away with faking it. Pluto is a hard taskmaster, but it will also give you that which no one can take away.

The positive expression through Pluto is a willingness, a grace that you accept, a calmness that allows you to transform and function. It takes you deep inside your soul and subconscious and brings forth that which is already within you. Pluto enables you to connect with yourself and grow.

The negative expression through Pluto is an intensity that can lead to destruction or death. It can create a loss of balance, getting completely out of kilter and becoming obsessive and willful.

Pluto exemplifies the law of retribution—whatever process or behavior you set forth you will receive back in spades. Not just in action but intent.

Pluto Retrograde

Pluto is generational. During its long revolution, many people will be born within each of its aspects. If Pluto is in retrograde motion, which it is for about six months of the year, half of the population will be born with a retrograde Pluto. This group of people is not necessarily going to act according to the rest of the group. These individuals will, sooner or later, stand out within that generation. They will either be famous or infamous.

Pluto Through the Signs

When Pluto stations in a sign during each generational period, it occasionally moves back or forward one sign for a few months. Always check your birth chart to see exactly where Pluto is placed.

Since Pluto was not discovered until 1930 and takes more than two centuries to fully transit through all twelve signs, it is difficult to observe the scope of its influence over time given the current human lifespan. We can only look back at how the world evolved in earlier generations and anticipate how it will manifest for those born under its influences in future generations.

PLUTO IN ARIES (1822–1853, 2068–2098)

The last time Pluto transited Aries was in the nineteenth century. During this time, we saw progress in railroad development, countries fighting for independence, movements toward abolishing slavery, and many advances in medicine and industry. It presents a time for leadership, political changes, revolutionary thinking, and technological advancements.

In this placement, individuals are impatient, independent, adventurous, and energetic. They take the initiative and will act ardently, sometimes before thinking things through.

PLUTO IN TAURUS (1853–1884)

The most memorable and perhaps most important aspect of Pluto in Taurus is that those born in this era left a valuable legacy: the birth of psychiatry. During Pluto's transit in Taurus, the world was influenced by eminent people such as Sigmund Freud and his student Carl Jung.

The generation born with this evolving concept saw medicine take a new step—the introduction of the body-mind connection. This concept, which took many years to evolve and be accepted, will be more prevalent for those with this placement. They will be focused on balance.

The acquisition of personal wealth may also be lucrative to those with this placement.

PLUTO IN GEMINI (1884–1914)

Pluto in Gemini is a collector of information. It produces communication and expression. This was an era of communicating, talking about, and introducing.

While Pluto was in Gemini, the world began to shrink. Airplanes were bringing countries closer together, which allowed people to visit other continents. The automobile shortened the distance between towns and states. The world was suddenly as close as our doorstep.

Relationships that spark thinking and ideas, and new forms to express them, may evolve during this placement.

PLUTO IN CANCER (1914–1939)

During the transit of Pluto in Cancer, the United States isolated itself from the rest of the world under the guise of "patriotism." The results would be a war that would send men to places and experiences they were ill prepared to face. The US also suffered an economic and emotional depression that would unite people in a common cause.

For those with Pluto in Cancer, emotions and intuitions rise to the surface where they can be either heightened or displaced.

PLUTO IN LEO (1939–1957)

When Pluto was in Leo, dictators became prominent, and there was a struggle for world power. That was exemplified by two wars: World War II and the Korean War. The sneak attack on Pearl Harbor and the autocratic regimes of European dictators, which allowed them to do as they pleased, illustrate the negative side of the authoritarian quality of Pluto in Leo.

Individuals with this placement can be either power hungry or ambitious for the good of society.

PLUTO IN VIRGO (1957–1972)

During this period, people stopped surrendering themselves to physicians and became interested in vitamins and organic food—the self-help concept was born. Society adopted an attitude of cleanliness, whether at home, in restaurants, hospitals, or cities. New laws and ordinances were instituted to protect food and water. This was an era that advocated purity and all things unadulterated.

Those born with Pluto in Virgo make excellent nurses,

doctors, healers, and even chefs and innkeepers. They are careful and meticulous, caught up in all that is soothing and clean, maintaining the beauty in simplicity.

PLUTO IN LIBRA (1972–1984)

Pluto in Libra signaled not only a need for equality, symmetry, and balance but also dealt with equilibrium. This was very relevant to partnerships. Pluto in Libra made sure that the egos of the partners in a relationship were equal, making sure that one did not weaken or overpower the other. Without respect and trust for a partner, there is no advancement.

During this time, relationships, marriage, and unions came to the forefront. The divorce rate was significantly increasing, and society started to believe that it was easier to discard a partner than to work out problems. A differentiation was made between a union created by two people and a simple, interacting relationship in which people communicate. This era demonstrated a lack of truth, a lack of reality, and a lack of solid interpersonal relationships. Marriage suffered the worse for it.

Those born with Pluto in Libra need harmony in their relationships, yet they often put their relationships to the test.

PLUTO IN SCORPIO (1984–1995)

Pluto rules Scorpio, so for every sunny disposition, there is a dark side of the personality that is usually kept hidden.

The beginning of this transit brought tension and deterioration. Everything turned to dust, everything disintegrated. Talent was questioned, and the only way to survive was to make sure you were good at what you were doing and not taking it for granted. You had to work hard and hone your craft, talent, or profession because if you didn't master it, you would lose it.

Those born with Pluto in Scorpio carry, in their subconscious, the need to clean up. Not just cleaning up the planet but cleaning up the inner self. In discovering the power within, in touching the spirit without labeling it, there will be self-esteem and the energy to keep illness at bay.

Pluto in Scorpio is a generation of powerful egos. And *ego* is not a dirty word. Everybody has an ego. Once the ego is recognized, fortified, and overcome, it can be eliminated.

PLUTO IN SAGITTARIUS (1995–2008)

Sagittarius is ruled by Jupiter, and Jupiter deals with relating. Jupiter gives Sagittarius a cognitive ability, and Pluto rules the collective unconscious. This generation cares about their fellow man. They can see things from a global perspective, cross cultures, and embrace the foreigner. Pluto in Sagittarius can formulate a brand-new human community in which the fellow man is understood. It is a small Earth, and man is more powerful, intelligent, and able to deal with people when he can understand and accept all religions, languages, and customs. Respect can finally surface for those things that we don't know or understand. In this placement, there is a desire to explore and discover, to expand learning, and to access information, which the growth of the internet helped provide.

PLUTO IN CAPRICORN (2008–2024)

The last time Pluto was in Capricorn was during the time leading up to the signing of the Declaration of Independence and when the United States began its fight against British rule. Shades of this are present in this returning transit, as power struggles are emerging within many countries among people and with their governments.

This generation focuses on business, government, power, ambition, and the fight for transformation between the old and the new. Those with this placement are organized and disciplined. They possess sharp and strategic minds, are driven and determined, and are technologically savvy. They also thrive in business and politics.

PLUTO IN AQUARIUS (2024–2044)

Aquarius is a humanitarian sign that embraces and advances social change. The last time Pluto was in Aquarius occurred during both the American and French Revolutions. Citizens fought for freedom and a new type of government that would protect the rights of its people. These same issues are likely to resurface again, bringing about changes in society, politics, belief systems, and critical thinking. Changes to social structures and relationships among people may be apparent and, hopefully, for the better. Those born in this generation will be creative, diverse, and open-minded and interested in diversity, tolerance, and human rights.

PLUTO IN PISCES (2044–2068)

Pisces is a deeply emotional sign, sensitive and intuitive. Those with Pluto in Pisces are tapped into the human psyche, both on a therapeutic level—making them excellent psychotherapists—and on a spiritual level. They may also possess psychic abilities, an uncanny ability to understand human nature, and healing powers. Their acute sensitivity and empathy can be influential in creating positive mental health changes, greater self-awareness, and the promotion of self-help practices for personal benefit and societal health and unity.

Pluto Through the Houses

PLUTO IN THE FIRST HOUSE

This placement calls for the native to become aware of the changes and extremes that his ego will undergo. If he becomes timid and afraid, he will suffer personality wounds. If he becomes overbearing, rejection will destroy his confidence. Balance is the lesson Pluto calls for in this house.

PLUTO IN THE SECOND HOUSE

In this house, Pluto carries the memory and fears of the miser. If the native learns to acquire, share, enjoy, and not hoard, he will keep the flow of prosperity going. If he becomes self-absorbed, he will have to reconstruct his financial life repeatedly until the correct approach can overcome his negative tactics.

PLUTO IN THE THIRD HOUSE

The house of communication works subtly, but it allows the native to use writing, painting, and other forms of expression to release thoughts from a depth he might not understand. There is an ease of thinking that makes for mental power. The native can either displace energy in a healthy manner or, like a pressure cooker, blow unexpectedly.

PLUTO IN THE FOURTH HOUSE

Pluto destroys the roots, hoping we will re-root. Dependent Cancers with this placement often have a great deal to work out with their mothers. A homelife of peace and tranquility eludes this person until he has set a foundation of love and selflessness.

PLUTO IN THE FIFTH HOUSE

Ruled by the Sun, this placement becomes a powerhouse. A word of caution—this power requires a great deal of strength to handle. Without restraint, it can lead to all kinds of excesses. Gentle, loving parents can handle unusual children. The rewards acquired by this position are of a grand scale.

PLUTO IN THE SIXTH HOUSE

Pluto's depth allows this position to tap a knowing that is helpful in the care of others. Psychologists or other mental caregivers usually have a strong Mercury/Pluto aspect. The need to serve is present, but it must be as a joyous giver, or those around this person will recognize the façade. This position makes for a hardworking individual whose health is contingent on releasing the energies of the central nervous system.

PLUTO IN THE SEVENTH HOUSE

Relationships, of which marriage can be the most important, are difficult, as the individual is being asked to withstand the onslaught of partners' thoughts and actions. Knowing what your partner is all about and still loving him might take all the power you possess. Corporate lawyers with this marker can conduct mediations and other legal matters successfully, as they can see both sides of the coin.

PLUTO IN THE EIGHTH HOUSE

This position has always been associated with death, the ultimate change. The native can create change with this aspect since only after a rebirth can we progress. The alternative is not to use these energies until one has degenerated into a physical illness or the darkness of the mind. To reach self-mastery is a victory that must be undertaken alone. The rewards are extraordinary strength and a fearless attitude.

PLUTO IN THE NINTH HOUSE

In this house, the mind can go deep into the subconscious and explore the "source," such as reincarnation or other beliefs. Unfortunately, it can also lead to a fear that produces fanatics or people who force their beliefs on others.

PLUTO IN THE TENTH HOUSE

The inherent struggle in this position can swing the native from being a recluse to being before the public. Success is attained by hard work and mastery. The willingness to share knowledge, to have patience with others, and to act with diplomacy result in rewards.

PLUTO IN THE ELEVENTH HOUSE

Pluto will attract all measure of help, so be careful of the source. Choosing friends and activities wisely is important, or you can find yourself dragged through the mud. The high level of Pluto can produce a much-admired or followed leader. Objectives and goals are achieved with a little help from friends.

PLUTO IN THE TWELFTH HOUSE

This placement, at its best, creates precognition. The native seems to have foreknowledge that can engender inspiration or misery. Feelings of confinement can be transcended by serving others as opposed to serving the ego. The talents of past lives can emerge as a source for advancement, regardless of the level of education in this life.

7

Planetary Relationships and Movement

ASPECTS

An aspect is an angle formed by two or more planets in relationship to each other. Collectively, these various aspects bring a chart to life.

Aspects are opportunities, some of which are difficult, some of which are frustrating, some of which are easy, and some of which are great. An aspect creates a potential—it is energy, and what you choose to do with this energy is entirely up to you; you make it either positive or negative.

There are many different aspects: squares, oppositions, conjunctions, trines, sextiles, quincunx, grand trines, grand crosses, and T-squares. Some of these are hard aspects, meaning that they present challenges but can inevitably produce more powerful or strengthening effects. Some are soft aspects, meaning that their influence is easy and free-flowing.

□ SQUARE

If two planets in your chart are 90 degrees apart, they form a square. A square is a powerful position. Without squares in your chart, you're never going to get off your duff and get anything done. A square is blocked energy, but it also creates a need to work things out. It is a hard aspect, but it has significance in a chart because it is an energizer.

Each square carries within it a quality that must be reconciled. It is the type of quality that makes you better as you get older. If you look at any chart of a successful person, you are sure to find squares.

☍ OPPOSITION

When two planets are 180 degrees apart, they form an opposition. *Opposition* means just that—two planets opposing each other. It is also a hard aspect.

An opposition has a midpoint where the qualities of these two planets can be reconciled. When planets oppose each other, they are polarizing, each representing the extreme end of the same polarity.

An opposition is an opportunity for objectivity. It allows you to see someone else's side of the picture in balance with your perspective. The keyword for an opposition is *objectivity*. Objectivity makes us aware of things we are often too close to see in an unbiased fashion. We are usually the worst judges of ourselves. Although we project ourselves into the world with a certain attitude or set of personal intentions, the world is often picking up something else. With an opposition, we can begin to gain awareness and understand cause and effect. We are given an objectivity that we don't ordinarily possess.

A chart with three or more oppositions is considered a medical chart. It usually means there is going to be hell to pay, most likely at the physical level. Too many oppositions make for a sick person. If that is the case in your chart, it's important to work to reconcile these polarities. That can be accomplished with a change of attitude.

☌ CONJUNCTION

A conjunction occurs when two planets come together within a few degrees of each other (it can be up to 10 degrees, depending on the power of the planet). A conjunction is considered a hard aspect.

Conjunctions often occur when two planets are within the same constellation. They can also be in different constellations as long as the distance between those planets is less than 10 degrees.

Because it produces power, a conjunction demands that you work through these planets at the same time. When a planet transits close to another planet and triggers it, it is called an *approach*. An approach is a powerful combination because it has a relay or domino effect—the planet that triggers the first triggers the second. It is a position of power and commands attention.

Conjunctions often produce overbearing or demanding people.

△ TRINE

A trine consists of three planets placed 120 degrees from one another. Trines are considered lucky and beneficial. When they occur in a chart, they create a smoothness, a kind of agility in the personality. Learning is easier, speaking is easier, performing is easier—it is as though there is a balance between intellect and emotion.

A trine indicates that you develop and function with the type of ease and harmony that produces creativity. You feel as if things are coming easily to you.

If your chart is full of trines, it can become problematic because it produces laziness. You feel as if you don't have to work for anything. It requires an individual to use those aspects so that laziness can be overcome.

If you combine a trine and a square, it creates a real dynamo. A square gives you energy, and a trine gives you luck—that's a surefire combination for success. It will give you the energy and creative impetus to get your ideas up off the drawing board.

* SEXTILE

A sextile is an aspect created by two planets 60 degrees from each other. This is a soft aspect, not as easy as the trine but ever so compatible.

What lies in a sextile is a chance. Two planets in a sextile aspect can easily be reconciled to produce opportunity. If you have a sextile in your chart, it is entirely up to you whether you work with the opportunity or ignore it.

ASPECT RELATIONSHIPS

When you have a natal chart created professionally or via computer, in addition to the wheel, an aspect grid may also be included (see page 46 for an example). The grid displays aspect relationships at the time of your birth in an easy-to-read format.

Make a note of the specific aspect relationships in your chart and use the following guide for the meaning of each aspect.

Aspects to the Sun

(Given the proximity of these planets, conjunctions are the only aspects made between Sun/Venus and Sun/Mercury.)

Sun ☌ Moon—A psychological orphan. The native will likely have to deal with the male or the female quality within himself from a personal point of view instead of from the perspective of his parents.

Sun △/* Moon—There was a great deal of harmony between one's parents at the time of conception leading to peace within this native.

Sun □ Moon—The native was born into a household where Mom and Dad were jockeying for position or simply didn't get along, causing inner conflict for this individual.

Sun ☌ Moon—Personal harmony must be worked out because it did not exist between the parents at the time of the native's birth.

Sun ☌ Mercury—The native communicates well and listens to himself.

Sun ☌ Venus—Self-love is an essential factor in the development of this personality—more than likely, self-love was not taught.

Sun ☌ Mars—The native possesses a great deal of energy and can be impulsive.

Sun △/* Mars—Deliberate and agile, the native works toward success. The energy in this female is attractive to males.

Sun □ Mars—Frustrated and willful, the native possesses a violent attitude that can lead to accidents or cruel acts.

Sun ☍ Mars—Irritable and angry, this personality becomes demanding and bossy. Females with this aspect are prone to be competitive.

Sun ☌ Jupiter—This aspect brings the ability to understand and relate to oneself. It also allows an understanding of the law of cause and effect.

Sun △/* Jupiter—Naturally attuned to the laws of the universe, the native is basically healthy. A favorable aspect for those in the medical field.

Sun □ Jupiter—Dishonest and willing to ride on the coattails of others, which can create an uncertain and unhealthy atmosphere. Honesty can help release stress and prevent health problems.

Sun ☍ Jupiter—This challenging aspect tends to overinflate self-importance. It could lead to overeating or overspending.

Sun ☌ Saturn—Indicates unfinished business. The native should take his status in the world seriously. There is something he must personally do and develop a sense of responsibility for it.

Sun △/* Saturn—This native doesn't challenge. He loves to work, does it well, and keeps his goals in sight, no matter how tough the road may be.

Sun □ Saturn—Epitomizes "self-fulfilling prophecy." The native is negative and fearful and, eventually, hardens. He receives what he gives. His body will become rigid and painful.

Sun ☌ Saturn—This aspect gives the native a chance to see what his attitudes can produce. He will attract people who will "do him one better" and force him to deal with his egocentricity.

Sun ☌ Uranus—Prophetic but untimely, the native must learn discretion. His strong will can lead to impulsiveness. The female finds her femininity a handicap.

Sun △/* Uranus—The forces of the collective unconscious come to the foreground. The personality is independent, original, and unconventional, but not suitable for intimacy.

Sun □ Uranus—This aspect is challenging to live with. The native can be impulsive, rude, and rebellious. His life will take sudden changes, some of which will go nowhere.

Sun ☍ Uranus—This native's life is subject to unexpected and uncontrollable conditions. He will be a victim of the whims or wills of others. He must learn to roll with the punches.

Sun ☌ Neptune—A misunderstood personality. The male appears to be romantic or mystical but is, in fact, lazy. The female comes across as a "whatever you want me to be" type, who still holds to her own agenda.

Sun △/* Neptune—Whatever talents have been amassed through past lives will surface. This native is a multitalented person that can excel in any field and have great staying power.

Sun □ Neptune—The native must serve or sacrifice. Past-life debts are to be collected.

Sun ☍ Neptune—This native "can't see the forest for the trees." Others will bring disappointment through unstable and chaotic situations. The native must learn to let go and avoid obsessive patterns of behavior.

Sun ☌ Pluto—Power in the rawest conditions. Negative views will produce infamy, but a positive attitude will attain the highest position within one's environment.

Sun △/* Pluto—Success will come. Strength and self-awareness cut a path toward achieving one's personal goals.

The ability to empower others attracts support and admiration.

Sun □ Pluto—Negative but strong-willed, this individual can be ruthless and egotistical. He can draw the worst of the underworld.

Sun ☍ Pluto—The danger of giving his power away to partners and associates is his emotional pitfall. This can lead to brutality or jealousy that makes him self-destructive.

Aspects to the Moon
Moon ☌ Mercury—This person can't hold his tongue. He can be a gossip or engage in condemnation to his detriment unless he becomes disciplined.

Moon △/* Mercury—This native is smooth thinking and an agile communicator. His brain is in gear before he speaks. He thinks on his feet and shows coordination between emotions and logic.

Moon □ Mercury—The objective of this native is to feel and think in harmony. He could bring troubles to himself through the written word.

Moon ☍ Mercury—This native doesn't hold back his opinion—he'll give it whether he's asked to or not. The results are that he will suffer in kind and the payback hurts.

Moon ☌ Venus—Love is in the air! When one love dies, another is waiting in the wings for this individual. Endowed physical beauty gives the native an opportunity to choose between love and the magnetic attraction of beauty.

Moon △/* Venus—Pleasant, sedate, and orderly, this native can acquire financial security in an artistic environment.

Moon □ Venus—Sloppy, especially with the feelings of others, this native has little or no knowledge of sisterhood.

Moon ☍ Venus—This aspect brings objectivity to the native. By observing the actions of others, the native realizes what he has brought upon himself. This can help overcome lovelessness.

Moon ☌ Mars—This aspect creates a bad temper and volatile situations. It also means that although a mother might have attended to this child responsibly and well, she might not have bonded as well as she could have.

Moon △/* Mars—Energy plus controlled emotions make for ease of actions and a great lover. Vitality and recuperative powers improve healing.

Moon □ Mars—An aggressive, self-centered character who will use the opposite sex for personal gratification. He will carry over into his life what his angry mother provided.

Moon ☍ Mars—Use restraint or suffer. This native will attract what he hates most. Emotional upheavals will be constant irritations that can only be overcome by patience and a loving attitude.

Moon ☌ Jupiter—A guardian angel is at work—whatever this native touches turns to gold. There is protection bestowed upon him that makes for a safe life. The native must not allow food to be his companion.

Moon △/* Jupiter—The ability to believe in oneself brings success. This, coupled with the assistance of others, makes for shared joy. The environment supports all endeavors.

Moon □ Jupiter—Control over diet or other indulgences is a must. Relating to others can overcome the narcissistic attitude of the native.

Moon ☍ Jupiter—The law of cause and effect is at work here. The native attracts what he projects even when he is not conscious of the action. His secret heart is revealed.

Moon ☌ Saturn—This frustrating and challenging aspect has the native in the grip of payback. Feeling sorry for himself will cause him to find himself alone. Mother did little or no nurturing, so he must be careful not to make others pay for this.

Moon △/* Saturn—Responsibility for accomplishments is key in this aspect. The native will take his family, job, and public duty seriously. He can withstand aloneness while serving others.

Moon □ Saturn—This aspect signifies a cold, complicated relationship with the mother. To overcome inherent fear and depression, this native needs to cultivate as much love as he can.

Moon ☌ Saturn—This aspect provides a chance to overcome the rigidity that Saturn imposes. Materialism is exciting and can provide many things as long as it is not handled in a cold and unresponsive way.

Moon ☌ Uranus—This aspect has difficulty relating to Mother, so early training is not established well. If he is lucky, intuition will prevent the native from creating more problems than he can handle. If not, the body pays.

Moon △/* Uranus—Potential for genius. Mental capacities and intuition combine to produce a creative and far-reaching individual who can adapt to sudden changes.

Moon □ Uranus—Unstable and willful, this person can create impossible relationships. Not successful at parenting, since nurturing requires calm, consistent, and loving acts that are difficult for this native to perform.

Moon ☍ Uranus—This ambitious and energetic native must be careful of his goals and who he enlists in his pursuits. The wrong people can influence him or support his willfulness, which can result in sorrow.

Moon ☌ Neptune—This sensitive and emotionally responsive native can overload. The diagnoses of health issues are unclear, as he seldom shows symptoms. Drugs are a problem since he poisons easily. The best medicine is sleep.

Moon △/* Neptune—Psychic abilities abound. The native must learn to protect himself since he cannot tolerate friction and chaos. Music, drama, and writing release the creative side of this personality.

Moon □ Neptune—The family, particularly Mother, may suffer from many afflictions, leaving this native with many insecurities and limitations. Until this personality develops a willingness to act, he will not acquire self-confidence.

Moon ☍ Neptune—This person must take a leap of faith to conquer the fears that cause his limitations. He must keep his head on straight and overcome the doubts that surface whenever he overthinks things.

Moon ☌ Pluto—This powerful aspect requires discipline to prevent takeovers. Mother, while influential, is a presence that should be diminished for a while so that this native can discover himself. This is an excellent aspect for a psychologist since it allows this person to become attuned to the needs of others.

Moon △/* Pluto—This aspect brings a sense of survival that overcomes any event. This native can rise above the impossible. This comes not from luck but from strength.

Moon □ Pluto—Patience and tolerance must be learned from others or else this individual will find himself alone and unsupported. Emotional upheavals will be part of his life.

Moon ☍ Pluto—An attraction to a powerful partner will have many ramifications, whether good or bad. Emotional ties can lead to unorthodox liaisons. Even when misunderstood, this native attracts others to him.

Aspects to Mercury
(Given the proximity of these planets, the only aspects made between Mercury and Venus are conjunction and sextile.)

Mercury ☌ Venus—Charming and mannered, this refined and artistic individual will be offended by coarse or crass communications.

Mercury * Venus—There is just enough ability for this native to be friendly, sociable, and pleasant—but don't expect much more.

Mercury ☌ Mars—Mentally aggressive, this native can become argumentative, sarcastic, and blunt, which, unless tempered by thought, will turn off many people.

Mercury △/* Mars—A clever fellow with a quick mind and wit. His sense of reason and mental agility makes for a fine student of any abstract subject.

Mercury ☐ Mars—A bad temper needs to be overcome or accidents will occur. Irritability will affect the nervous system of this native, and the body will pay the price with muscle spasms.

Mercury ☍ Mars—If he uses his energies well, this native can persevere and reach his goals. If not, he will find himself a victim of bad press.

Mercury ☌ Jupiter—A philosophical mind and a generous soul. This native will be paid in kind. If he is not lazy or stubborn, he will enjoy abundance.

Mercury △/* Jupiter—Good judgment and awareness of possibilities will help this native to cope with even the most difficult of circumstances. He keeps the faith and reaps the benefits of positive thinking.

Mercury ☐ Jupiter—The native with this aspect cannot keep his promises. His intentions are good, but he bites off more than he can chew. He can procrastinate and become physically ill when his goals are not reached.

Mercury ☍ Jupiter—Depending on the polarities, this aspect can produce stubbornness and biased opinions or good judgment and cooperation.

Mercury ☌ Saturn—A serious personality whose hard work, coupled with ambition, can lead to success but cost him the joys of life.

Mercury △/* Saturn—This native takes the responsibility of education seriously. He has an excellent memory and practical attitudes that result in success in his profession. He will make sure his portfolio is up to date.

Mercury ☐ Saturn—Negative thinking is natural but causes depression. This native must work to clear his mind of the negative to avoid and overcome the psychosomatic conditions that can afflict him.

Mercury ☍ Saturn—Separation seems to plague this life. Loneliness becomes the result of distrust and suspicion. This can be overcome by efforts to reach out.

Mercury ☌ Uranus—When the energies of this aspect are harnessed, it creates a superior mind. But let those same energies run wild and it will bring destruction.

Mercury △/* Uranus—This aspect is quick and ahead of the pack, but can lose patience with those who are not similarly endowed. Individuality can be expressed well through writing.

Mercury □ Uranus—The mental forces are strong, intuitive, and prophetic here but this native is seldom understood. He will not be taken seriously unless he harnesses his mental energies and develops tact.

Mercury ☍ Uranus—Thoughts are erratic and difficult to explain. This native will display impatience, which compounds his nervousness and sometimes confuses communications.

Mercury ☌ Neptune—Neptune creates inaccuracies in mental function. The objective is to focus on the tried-and-true and harden to external stimuli.

Mercury △/* Neptune—This aspect presents options that can foster dreams, visions, and the creative mind with which to implement them. The native enters the void and returns inspired.

Mercury □ Neptune—This position creates an illusion that will eventually undress the native. He must take seriously, and depend on, his mental faculties instead of picking someone else's mind.

Mercury ☍ Neptune—What we don't see in ourselves, others do. There is a great deal of suffering from the reactions of others to a wishy-washy attitude.

Mercury ☌ Pluto—This aspect is the signature of psychologists, psychiatrists, and anyone else who deals with the collective unconscious.

Mercury △/* Pluto—This agile mind can absorb and retain information to everyone's surprise. He can move groups with his logic and influence with his emotions.

Mercury □ Pluto—This powerful aspect requires tempering, as it can lead to workaholic types. This is a person whose intensity will burn him out.

Mercury ☍ Pluto—Insight and inner strength help to smooth a conflict that is ever-present in this native. The world will see him as a rock while he longs for tender love.

Aspects to Venus

Venus ☌ Mars—Love or lust—which is it? This aspect will challenge the native until he can distinguish between the two and act accordingly.

Venus △/* Mars—One hand washes the other. Cooperation, love, and kindness add up to tranquility. The success will be seen in matters of love and money.

Venus □ Mars—The responses of this native tend to feed cruel and violent acts. He must learn to control himself or he will be battered.

Venus ♂ Mars—This native has to be aware of the mood swings that trigger his responses. The practice of self-control is his best ally.

Venus ☌ Jupiter—The grace bestowed on this aspect takes the native far both socially and professionally. This aspect can also produce a detached but cultured personality.

Venus △/* Jupiter—This position gives the native a softer approach to others. He will be aware of others' needs, and while he prospers in all areas, he will also share.

Venus □ Jupiter—The need for controlling what would ordinarily be considered good fortune shows up in this aspect. This abundance can lead to overindulgences that will be manifested in the body.

Venus ♂ Jupiter—This native must not indulge in vanity or wastefulness at the cost of future security.

Venus ☌ Saturn—This conjunction brings a fear that can prohibit giving or receiving love from others. It will take courage to open up.

Venus △/* Saturn—This native has the insight to endure whatever life brings without losing faith. Maturity will reward this individual with caring people and solid relationships.

Venus □ Saturn—This aspect brings the inability to understand the meaning of self-love, which results in disappointments in relationships and an eventual sense of loneliness.

Venus ☍ Saturn—This aspect is hard to live with, but if one can give love to those who are unloving, this karma can be overcome.

Venus ☌ Uranus—There are other fish in the ocean, so this native goes looking for them. He can't tell the difference between independence and indifference.

Venus △/* Uranus—This magnetic personality needs to be discreet. He can attract all measures of money and exciting love affairs. He can also find himself starting over—not to worry, he can!

Venus □ Uranus—Take one step at a time and be willing to redirect. Uranus is a magnet, but in this aspect, there is no guarantee that what is attracted has longevity or is beneficial.

Venus ☍ Uranus—Don't fence anyone in or they will

leave, whether business or marital partners or children. Watch finances.

Venus ☌ Neptune—This position creates instability in love affairs. While reality is not as romantic as love, on a higher plane, reality is more reliable.

Venus △/* Neptune—The good bestowed upon the native is not easily recognized. The sensitive nature of this individual loves music and tranquil surroundings. He doesn't do well in the corporate world.

Venus □ Neptune—This aspect can be overcome by being loving toward all in a universal sense. It does not work well on a one-to-one basis. Care must be given to financial resources or others will help themselves.

Venus ☍ Neptune—Doing the unpopular thing for the right reasons can put this native on the road to sacrifice. He needs to take off the rose-colored glasses and strengthen his resolve. Being alone can sometimes lead to insight.

Venus ☌ Pluto—This aspect brings power and strength to the love nature that can result in insatiable lust at any cost. The positive side is a nature that transcends all superficial barriers.

Venus △/* Pluto—The quiet but powerful magnetism of

Pluto ensures the abundance of money, love, respect, opportunities, or whatever else the native might need to succeed.

Venus □ Pluto—This aspect can produce an unethical personality that will eventually be exposed. Loneliness will be his companion until he learns to respect and love others.

Venus ☍ Pluto—This native can find himself in a love triangle, and he will lose. Loving without vested interest will be far more rewarding and safer.

Aspects to Mars

Mars ☌ Jupiter—The energy produced by this combination can be either dangerous or inspired. If not disciplined, it's merely risk-taking. If controlled, physical stress can be avoided.

Mars △/* Jupiter—The expansion of Jupiter can bring an abundance of energy to the athlete or mental prowess to the philosophical mind. The ease of this combination allows for the completion of all tasks.

Mars □ Jupiter—Depending on the rest of the chart, this aspect can undo the native. He either wants too much of everything or acts in a hit-and-run manner. This aspect requires pondering and self-awareness to make profitable use of these energies.

Mars ☍ Jupiter—One can lose sight of what and when is enough, which can be physically damaging or financially dangerous. The intolerance toward others makes for a lonely path.

Mars ☌ Saturn—This aspect creates frustration and the inability to push forward no matter how much energy is spent. Power will elude the native.

Mars △/* Saturn—Success in business and a willingness to work for it produce good results. The discipline of Mars leads to a steady and fruitful life.

Mars □ Saturn—This aspect creates frustration and a dampening of energy.

Mars ☍ Saturn—The push/pull of energy quiets the antagonism. Conquer and complete the "unfinished business" brought by Saturn and karmic debts will be paid.

Mars ☌ Uranus—The temperament of this native can lead to his demise. While he appears fearless, his impatience makes him dangerous. The most beneficial undertaking for this native is to care for others tirelessly.

Mars △/* Uranus—The correct use of this aspect makes for an exciting, adventurous character. He will be on the move looking for what's new in the world.

Mars □ Uranus—This aspect will quickly show the results of unwise decisions. The sudden violence that can erupt will leave no time for regrets. Through recklessness, the native draws and courts disaster.

Mars ☍ Uranus—This native will confront having to control the disruptive and bad-tempered people drawn to him. The situation can be diffused by learning not to react.

Mars ☌ Neptune—Neptune waters down the energies of Mars, leaving a frightened and sometimes disruptive personality. Self-actualization can bring about a responsible, disciplined, and advanced individual.

Mars △/* Neptune—An active but hidden guardian angel is at work. Dreams are fulfilled, while distractions are ineffective.

Mars □ Neptune—Clear, direct, and honest communications are a must. Actions backed by good motives are the way to avoid difficulties. Alcohol is detrimental to the mind and body.

Mars ☍ Neptune—This native can be duped by others. Deception and deceit must be avoided. Making sacrifices for others can be of benefit.

Mars ☌ Pluto—Gentle, loving actions succeed where bullish destructive actions fail.

Mars △/* Pluto—This self-reliant and self-motivated athlete or corporate head achieves. This aspect also shows occult abilities.

Mars □ Pluto—Controlling the tiger within can avoid a violent, internal struggle. Be careful!

Mars ☍ Pluto—The native must be alert to the influences of others or he will fall into a path of destruction.

Aspects to Jupiter

Jupiter ☌ Saturn—This native can be effective when wise enough to get the hang of his life's expanding path.

Jupiter △/* Saturn—This aspect doesn't let you kid yourself. The native works for what he desires and achieves.

Jupiter □ Saturn—This aspect calls for the native to face his responsibilities. In not doing so, he can squander his talents and opportunities.

Jupiter ☍ Saturn—Reclusive or outgoing? The choice will be made through the maturation process.

Jupiter ☌ Uranus—The ability to couple strong intuition with creative powers makes this combination forceful if not unconventional.

Jupiter △/* **Uranus**—The native attains whatever he pursues. Good fortune allows him to capitalize on all opportunities.

Jupiter □ **Uranus**—Patience will calm the irritability of this aspect. The mind is fast, and follow-through is spontaneous.

Jupiter ♂ **Uranus**—Religious pursuit will cause this native to challenge the dogma of established institutions. Judgment must be checked to see if it is trustworthy.

Jupiter ♂ **Neptune**—The emotions are on a roller-coaster ride. This aspect can have the native paying lip service when his courage fails.

Jupiter △/* **Neptune**—The chance to put together thought and action results in a sedate, kind, and almost mystical personality.

Jupiter □ **Neptune**—Curtail certain thoughts and actions or else fall into the hands of unscrupulous people.

Jupiter ♂ **Neptune**—Watch the body—it will pay for all lack of control. Stop depending on others; heal thyself.

Jupiter ♂ **Pluto**—A leader must attain self-mastery. Only then can he achieve with ease the recognition, admiration, and cooperation of others.

Jupiter △/* **Pluto**—This native has the strength to succeed no matter what. He must help himself as well as others.

Jupiter □ **Pluto**—This aspect doesn't assure one's power, which leads to constant testing. This can be a waste of time, bringing only self-deception.

Jupiter ☍ **Pluto**—The instability with which this native operates is testimony to his anxieties about his self-importance.

Aspects to Saturn

Saturn ☌ **Uranus**—This native usually shows only the tip of the iceberg. The danger lies in an unexpected reaction that can destroy all his accomplishments.

Saturn △/* **Uranus**—This native can distinguish the value of the old from the outmoded. He grows toward the new without offending.

Saturn □ **Uranus**—The way to freedom is to face responsibilities. When that is done, Uranus will drive this native.

Saturn ☍ **Uranus**—Security drawn from what is tried-and-true can lead to boredom. Avoid impulsive acts, for they will not remedy this situation. There could be many losses.

Saturn ☌ **Neptune**—Neptune can deepen fears, and

depression can lead to withdrawal. Facing limitations will lead to forward movement.

Saturn △/* Neptune—Psychic abilities can produce tangible results.

Saturn □ Neptune—Perhaps the hardest of aspects, this native endures irrational fears. Safety lies in acquiring a God-oriented philosophy.

Saturn ☌ Neptune—Striking a balance between spirituality and materialism can benefit this native. He will find himself having to choose continually.

Saturn ☌ Pluto—This native cannot handle superficial people or acts. His seriousness about life leads him to sort out what is truly important.

Saturn △/* Pluto—This slow, methodical, and trustworthy native will succeed in his endeavors but must not expect others to function as he does.

Saturn □ Pluto—The need to express individuality may cause pain and upheaval. Lessons will be passed on for the use of future generations.

Saturn ☌ Pluto—What is brought by this aspect to the native can be the greatest challenge of his life. To hang on, no matter how unfair, difficult, or trying, is to conquer the fear of all vulnerability.

Aspects to Uranus

Uranus ☌ Neptune—There is insecurity about personal freedom. Reform of social or personal conditions will be made. New drugs on the market might have adverse effects.

Uranus △/* Neptune—The realization that one has a spirit and the desire to express it occurs with this aspect. Those around might not understand or see the value. Go for it.

Uranus ☐ Neptune—Keep the mind healthy, whether by proper nutrition or a positive attitude. Avoid joining strange groups without investigating carefully. What is new is not necessarily good.

Uranus ☍ Neptune—Putting a handle on what this aspect can bring will require a great deal of grounding. The opportunity to rise above a boring life can lead to strange encounters. Be careful.

Uranus ☌ Pluto—This aspect prompts changes. It brings cleansing and healing of the environment, medicine, or one's psyche.

Uranus △/* Pluto—There will be a slow but methodical

exploration of one's life. The result will be changes, growth, and transformation. Karmic debts are being paid.

Uranus □ Pluto—This native is prone to upheaval and will not be able to stay put. Regeneration of the self becomes a must for survival.

Uranus ☍ Pluto—Life is filled with deception and upheaval. One must learn to take it in stride.

Aspects to Neptune

Neptune ☌ Pluto—An adventurous personality with unusual ideas and objectives.

Neptune △/* Pluto—Justice in all endeavors is key.

Neptune □ Pluto—Persevering, knowing what is right, and gently letting go of what is not will prevent falling into the wrong hands.

Neptune ☍ Pluto—It's time to clean closets and unload material or mental/psychological debris. Lighten the load and live.

Quincunx

A quincunx is a 150-degree angle between two planets. Since this aspect is 30 degrees short of being an opposition, it leaves you flapping in the breeze.

A quincunx creates a difficulty, an irritation, or a lack of harmony. It is called a *neurotic genius aspect*, which is not a bad thing. Oriental philosophy says that to polish a gem, there must be friction. In a quincunx, there is enormous friction. If you are grumpy, crabby, and not working out or reconciling your feelings, that's all you're ever going to be, and you will get stuck in your tracks. But if you use a quincunx well, the by-product of friction and discord will be harmony.

Grand Trine

When the three Sun Signs of each element (fire, earth, air, or water) are all in trine position to each other, it is called a *grand trine*. Although trines are considered lucky, a grand trine is also equated with laziness and a lackadaisical attitude.

Grand Cross

A grand cross is created by the four signs of any quadruplicity being in a square to one another. The "cross" is formed by the two sets of oppositions that intersect in the chart. A grand cross influences the mind-body connection of a chart. This is a difficult aspect to handle because, although it can be dynamic, it is also hard to keep this energy in balance. As they say, what doesn't kill you will make you stronger.

There are three types of grand crosses, each emphasizing the unique quality of either cardinal, fixed, or mutable:

Cardinal Grand Cross—The cardinal grand cross represents initiation and action, powerful energies that can destroy or create. It is will versus soul, reflecting where you have taken your soul, where you stand, and your status in this world.

Fixed Grand Cross—In the fixed grand cross, the strength of the body and mind will be challenged. To know oneself, be disciplined, and give to others requires a trust that individuals with this cross do not naturally possess. This is the embodiment of the paradox of "what you hold, you will lose; what you give, you will have."

Mutable Grand Cross—The mutable grand cross creates a nervous tension that is calling for change. One must give up, change, or release uncertainty. It is time to review, not criticize.

T-Square

Suppose one of the four planets was missing from a grand cross—you have an opposition and two squares, but there's an empty leg. So, instead of having four planets in square positions to one another, you only have three. That is what is called a *T-square*. And it is really going to throw you out of kilter.

The T-square can only be reconciled by the empty leg. The empty leg creates the ability to reconcile the other three planets, but not with ease. It is always a difficult situation when you have a T-square. It brings a lot of energy, but you must learn to use and direct that energy in a way that is advantageous to yourself and for the benefit of others. Although T-squares are challenging, they can, ultimately, show you the way. They keep your strength up. They are necessary for helping you accomplish short- and long-term goals.

TRANSITS

The day, hour, and place of your birth create your natal chart. That's a frozen moment of time that will not change. However, all the planets represented in your chart at the time of your birth have now moved on, each according to its own velocity. That movement is called a *separating aspect*. This is important because maturation occurs through the impact of planets as they continue to move—to transit.

That frozen moment of your birth is a recording of your innate and inherited traits, personality, and potential. The natal chart and its aspects are important because they form your foundation. Understanding what can be developed out of that foundation and how you handle this maturation will be influenced by transits.

To find out past, present, and future transits, you can consult the following resources:

- an ephemeris
- astrology websites, especially those with free chart creation (see the resources section for links)

- daily newspaper horoscopes (transits are often mentioned)
- a monthly astrology magazine or annual horoscope/book

Obtaining a chart of the current transits in your chart is easy, but interpreting them requires more advanced knowledge of astrology. Understanding current and near-future transits and their effect on your birth chart can help you plan and prepare for—or even avoid—decision-making, business transactions, personal commitments, purchases, and elective surgery and procedures.

You can dedicate time to learning more about astrology—particularly mundane (predictive) astrology—by purchasing a computerized report or consulting with a professional astrologer to examine your chart and discuss the influence of upcoming planetary trends.

Retrograde Transits

A retrograde is an apparent backward motion—a loss of velocity in comparison to Earth. The highest level of tension will occur when the planet appears to be stationary before retrograding. Each planet will carry a message and will affect your chart accordingly.

MERCURY RETROGRADE

This occurs three times a year, always in a different constellation. Depending on the placement, some Mercury retrograde periods will be easy to handle and others will be difficult. During these phases, all forms of communication will be delayed, misconstrued, lost. The signing of contracts or other types of commitments will be unclear or subject to change in the future. You will have wished you had read the small print. This is also a bad time to purchase anything electronic or mechanical unless you are replacing something that breaks down. Each Mercury retrograde period lasts for three weeks during each occurrence, accounting for almost ten weeks per year. Although frustrating, this is an appropriate time to relax, reevaluate, and reconnect.

VENUS RETROGRADE

Venus will be retrograding for six weeks, during which time there will be an effect on women at large. Venus rules beauty, so experimenting with a new hairstyle, hair color, or having cosmetic procedures is not recommended. Venus also rules relationships. It is best to avoid getting married or initiating a new relationship during this transit because the long-term outcome may prove disappointing.

MARS RETROGRADE

This occurs for ten weeks every two years. This cycle presents the opportunity to assess jobs or love affairs. If all is well, a direct Mars will not destroy the relationship. Staying on the job may lead to looking toward a promotion.

JUPITER RETROGRADE

Jupiter spends two and a half months retrograding. The point of retrograde varies from year to year, but the effects are influential to the chart. It is an opportunity to see if you are aware of how you relate to others. The retrograde will give feedback on the effects.

SATURN RETROGRADE

Saturn retrogrades for about four and a half months. You can be sure you will note it because it takes your energy and forces you to be patient. It asks that you sort out your responsibilities and apply yourself to worthwhile endeavors.

URANUS RETROGRADE

Uranus retrogrades for about five months. It provides an opportunity to review that new idea you thought was great. Will it work out? You can build a better mousetrap or work with time. This retrograde forces you to take a closer look at anything unconventional.

NEPTUNE RETROGRADE

Neptune retrogrades for about five months. Because it is in each house for fourteen years, it is important to understand the house in which it is retrograding. The fear that can surface during a Neptune retrograde can destroy the positive creativity of the individual.

PLUTO RETROGRADE

Pluto retrogrades for about six months. Its travel is slow and eccentric, causing great stress for the house it is occupying. The opportunity to rectify your goals is present, as Pluto provides a wealth of information.

Glossary

affliction: An unfavorable aspect to a planet in an astrological chart.

air signs: The three Sun Signs associated with mentality—Gemini, Libra, and Aquarius.

approach: When a planet transits close to another planet and triggers it.

ascendant: The sign of the Zodiac rising over the eastern horizon at the time of birth. Also referred to as the *rising sign.*

aspect: The relationship between planets measured in degrees. Some aspects are positive and some are not.

astrological chart: A diagram of the placement of planets in signs and houses of a pivotal, timed moment of inception such as a birth, marriage, or start of a business.

astrology: The art and science of analyzing human development and events by the effects of the position and movement of zodiacal signs and planets.

birth chart: A diagram of the placement of planets in signs and houses at a person's date and time of birth.

cardinal cross: A group of four signs—Aries, Cancer, Libra, and Capricorn—that are positioned in opposition to one another in the natural Zodiac and share similar characteristics of initiative and action.

collective unconscious: Term coined by psychologist Carl Jung that refers to the concept of a universal field or bank of knowledge that can be tapped by those who are psychically evolved.

conjunction: Two planets that occupy the same position or degree or are close to each other.

constellation: A band of stars in the universe. Twelve of these bands represent the twelve signs of the Zodiac.

cross: Four planets in opposition to each other that share certain dynamic qualities. There are three crosses—cardinal, fixed, and mutable. Also referred to as *quadruplicity* or *mode*.

cusp: The dividing line at which an astrological sign or house begins.

decan: One of three 10-degree segments of a 30-degree zodiacal Sun Sign.

descendant: The opposition point of the ascendant in an astrological chart occurring on the western horizon. Equal to the seventh house or sunset part of a day.

Dragon's Head / Dragon's Tail: See *Moon nodes*.

earth signs: The three Sun Signs associated with practicality and groundedness—Taurus, Virgo, and Capricorn.

ecliptic: The orbit of Earth and the apparent orbit of the Sun.

elements: Four elements—fire, earth, air, and water—each consisting of three signs that share similar characteristics. Also referred to as *triplicities*.

ephemeris: A reference guide that shows exact planetary positions for any day, month, or year.

esoteric astrology: The study of the symbolic meaning of the planets and signs.

fire signs: The three Sun Signs associated with enthusiasm and impulsiveness—Aries, Leo, and Sagittarius.

fixed cross: A group of four signs—Taurus, Leo, Scorpio, and Aquarius—that are positioned in opposition to one another in the natural Zodiac and share similar characteristics of determination and rigidity.

geocentric: The astrological perspective placing Earth, rather than the Sun, at the center of planetary movement.

glyph: A symbol that represents an astrological sign, planet, or aspect.

grand cross: An aspect formed by two sets of oppositions that create a square configuration in a chart, with each planet in the same quadruplicity (cardinal, mutable, or fixed).

grand trine: A triangle formed by three planets positioned 120 degrees from one another.

horoscope: See *astrological chart*.

houses: The twelve segments of an astrological chart.

imum coeli (IC): See *nadir*.

karma: The results that a person's actions bring upon himself during the whole of his existence.

mandala: The birth chart or horoscope.

medium coeli (MC): See *midheaven*.

midheaven: The upper meridian or noon position in an astrological chart. Occurs in the tenth house (also called *medium coeli*).

mode: See *cross*.

Moon nodes: The north and south points on the ecliptic where the Moon crosses it. The North Node is also called the *Dragon's Head*; the South Node is also called the *Dragon's Tail*.

mutable cross: A group of four signs—Gemini, Virgo, Sagittarius, and Pisces—that are positioned in opposition to one another in the natural Zodiac and share similar characteristics of adaptability and flexibility.

nadir: The lower meridian of an astrological chart or the fourth house (also called *imum coeli*).

natal chart: See *birth chart*.

native: The person associated with his or her specific birth chart.

North Node: See *Moon nodes*. Also referred to as the *Dragon's Head*.

opposition: Two planets that are in a 180-degree aspect to each other or opposing each other.

planets: The ten celestial bodies that influence astrology. The Sun (a star) and the Moon (a satellite of Earth) are considered planets in astrology.

polarity: Signs in opposition to each other within the Zodiac.

quadrant: one of four equal sections (quadrant of an astrological wheel), each containing three houses in sequence.

quadruplicity: See *cross*.

quincunx: Two planets that are in a 150-degree aspect to each other.

retrograde: The loss of velocity of a planet that makes it appear to be traveling backward.

rising sign: See *ascendant*.

separating aspect: The continuous movement of planets away from their positions at the time of birth.

sextile: Two planets that are in a 60-degree aspect to each other.

sign: The zodiacal constellation that any planet falls into in an astrological chart.

South Node: See *Moon nodes*. Also referred to as the *Dragon's Tail*.

square: Two planets that are in a 90-degree aspect to each other. Indicative of a difficulty that needs to be overcome.

Sun Sign: One of the twelve signs of the Zodiac, each embodying unique personality characteristics.

T-square: An aspect formed by the opposition of two planets and both square a third planet.

transit: The movement of a planet through a sign, or house, or over another planet.

trine: Three planets in a 120-degree aspect to each other. Usually indicates a harmonious situation.

triplicity: See *elements*.

water signs: The three Sun Signs associated with emotion and sensitivity—Cancer, Scorpio, and Pisces.

Zodiac: A belt of fixed stars that circles Earth, divided into twelve sections representing the constellations of Aries, Taurus, Gemini, Cancer, Leo, Virgo, Libra, Scorpio, Sagittarius, Capricorn, Aquarius, and Pisces.

GLYPH IDENTIFIER

♈	Aries	☉	Sun	□	Square
♉	Taurus	☽	Moon	☍	Opposition
♊	Gemini	☿	Mercury	☌	Conjunction
♋	Cancer	♀	Venus	△	Trine
♌	Leo	♂	Mars	✳	Sextile
♍	Virgo	♃	Jupiter	⚻	Quincunx
♎	Libra	♄	Saturn		
♏	Scorpio	♅	Uranus		
♐	Sagittarius	♆	Neptune		
♑	Capricorn	♇	Pluto		
♒	Aquarius	☊	North Node		
♓	Pisces	☋	South Node		
		ASC	Ascendant		
		MID	Midheaven		

Resources

All resources noted here have been compiled at press time and may be subject to change or availability. Since new programs and software become available regularly, there will be many more to choose from beyond what is listed here. The following resources should help you get started.

FREE NATAL CHARTS

To obtain or create an accurate natal chart, be sure you have your exact date, time, and place of birth.

- Astrodienst: https://www.astro.com
- Astro-Charts: https://astro-charts.com
- Astroseek: https://horoscopes.astro-seek.com/birth-chart-horoscope-online

COMPUTER SOFTWARE

There are several software programs available for purchase, but most are for professional astrologers and can be pricey. Some companies offer multiple programs covering Windows and Mac operating systems, and Android and iPhone apps.

- Matrix Software: https://www.astrologysoftware.com
- Astro Gold: https://www.astrogold.io
- Time Passages: https://www.astrograph.com/astrology-software
- Cosmic Patterns Software: https://www.astrosoftware.com

Index

About the Authors

ADA AUBIN, a Taurus, was a professional astrologer for over forty years. Born in Rincón, Puerto Rico, she moved with her family to New York as a child. After graduating high school, she met her husband, Frank, and they settled happily on Long Island, raising four children. During her thirties, a neighbor coaxed Ada into attending a lecture led by astrologer Lionel Day. She entered the class a skeptic and left inspired. As the daughter of a Presbyterian minister and Sunday school teacher, no one would have imagined that astrology would soon become her passion and career for decades to follow.

Ada wholeheartedly began studying astrology under the guidance of Mr. Day and other noted astrologers of the era. She attended astrology symposiums conducted through New York University and, in April 1973, received certification by the Astrologers' Guild of America.

In the ensuing years, Ada established a thriving, private astrology practice with a vast clientele across the U.S. and abroad. She lectured at Suffolk Community College, participated in numerous seminars, and led many astrology classes, culminating in the publication of *The Complete Book of Astrology*.

Ada passed away in her sleep on March 14, 2008, in Colorado. Known as "Grandma" to all her grandchildren's friends and classmates,

Ada left behind a long legacy of people who loved her and will miss her forever.

JUNE RIFKIN, a Pisces, is the author and coauthor of several books, including *Signature for Success: How Handwriting Can Influence Your Career, Your Relationships, and Your Life* (with Arlyn Imberman) and *The Everything Baby Name Book.* She is currently collaborating on a book on Tarot.

June has a master's degree in writing and publishing from Emerson College and has written several plays, including *Separation Anxiety,* published by Next Stage Press, and featured in the book *One on One: The Best Women's Monologues of the 21st Century.* She has also served as editor on other books, including *Churrasco: Grilling the Brazilian Way, Rebirth: The Journey of Pregnancy After a Loss,* and *Healing Your Child's Brain.*